8-23-73

The March to Magdala

THE ABYSSINIAN WAR
OF 1868

19TH CENTURY MILITARY CAMPAIGNS

General Editor Brian Bond

The March to Magdala
THE ABYSSINIAN WAR
OF 1868

by

FREDERICK MYATT

LEO COOPER · LONDON

First published in Great Britain 1970
by LEO COOPER LTD
47 Museum Street, London W.C.1

© 1970 Frederick Myatt

ISBN 0 85052 026 6

Printed in Great Britain
by Clarke, Doble & Brendon, Ltd. at Plymouth

1764525

CONTENTS

ILLUSTRATIONS

MAPS

INTRODUCTION AND
ACKNOWLEDGEMENTS

THE Abyssinian campaign took place during a period of considerable military activity in Europe, and there was thus no lack of expert professional interest in what was clearly going to be a difficult and testing operation. As it turned out there was comparatively little fighting. The real problem was logistical—how to maintain a considerable force penetrating deeply into an unknown and relatively barren country; it is with these administrative aspects of the campaign that this book is chiefly concerned.

The apparent inability of the British Army to maintain itself had been one of the most striking features of the Crimean War a few years previously and there was a good deal of apprehension—one might almost say anticipation—that the Abyssinian affair would collapse into similar chaos. Nor were these apprehensions unfounded. A good deal had been done in the previous ten years to streamline the British military machine, but in spite of this it is clear that no really effective system had been evolved by 1868. The initial arrangements were in fact grotesquely inefficient in many respects and it was only due to the on-the-spot efforts of a competent commander, ably seconded by staff officers of the calibre of the future Lord Roberts, that a shambles was averted.

In spite of early uncertainties however, the operation was a resounding success and did a good deal to restore Great Britain's status as a military power; in particular it demonstrated clearly

9

that her arm was long, and that no erring potentate, however remote, could flout her with impunity—an important consideration for a great colonial empire.

Apart from the administrative problems the campaign is interesting for its many modern aspects. Breech-loading weapons were used, as were searchlights, photography, the field telegraph, a specially constructed railway, and up-to-date condensers and pumps for the supply of water.

The actual British Army participation was comparatively small. The bulk of the force was Indian and only one incomplete cavalry regiment and four infantry battalions (one of which was employed on the lines of communication) came from the British service. Nevertheless British soldiers formed the bulk of the division which actually took Magdala so it is natural that they received most of the publicity. The campaign was almost the last appearance of the old, long-service army, and we must not begrudge them their final round of applause.

At the time of the campaign most British line regiments were known by their numbers. Some, however, including those employed in Abyssinia, had alternative titles which they used a good deal, and I have followed their lead in this book.

The provision of suitable maps proved something of a problem. It is no exaggeration to say that the main theatre of operations was four hundred miles long and a few furlongs wide; this makes it difficult to illustrate to scale—nor would the results be very illuminating. The maps are therefore restricted to a general one of Northern Abyssinia and a more detailed one of Magdala and its approaches, where the main actions took place. A complete schedule of marches and distances has been included as an appendix. The spelling of place and proper names follows the Official History, except in cases where a modern alternative is more easily recognized.

A great many people have contributed to this book. Mr D. W. King, OBE, Chief Librarian of the Ministry of Defence Library (Army and Central) and his staff have, as ever, been patient and helpful, and I am also indebted to Mr S. C. Sutton, CBE, Librarian of the India Office Library, and his staff for providing a great deal of material from their archives.

INTRODUCTION AND ACKNOWLEDGEMENTS

The Regimental Secretaries of the three British Regiments chiefly concerned, Colonel H. J. Darlington, OBE, DL, the King's Own Royal Border Regiment, Lieutenant-Colonel G. P. Gofton-Salmond, OBE, the Sherwood Foresters, and Major J. W. Davis, the Duke of Wellington's Regiment, have all offered advice and assistance of various kinds, as have Lieutenant-Colonel H. S. Francis, OBE, Curator of the Museum of the Corps of Royal Engineers, and Major R. St. G. G. Bartelot of the Royal Artillery Institution. Lieutenant-Colonel R. W. Armstrong of Regimental Headquarters the Royal Corps of Transport, Brigadier B. Burkin of the Royal Army Ordnance Corps Secretarial, and Brigadier C. E. T. Ince, CB, CBE, sometime head of the food supply staff, have also been most helpful.

I am grateful to Mr W. Y. Carman, FSA (Scotland), of the National Army Museum who found several of the old photographs for me, and to Stephen Bell and John Fynn who provided the excellent modern ones and from whose written account the short appendix on Magdala today is based.

The March to Magdala

THE ABYSSINIAN WAR
OF 1868

CHAPTER 1
An Unknown Land

In August 1867, Great Britain finally decided to despatch a military expedition into Abyssinia. There was, to be sure, no great enthusiasm on the part of the newly-elected Tory government to involve the country in a campaign which was likely to cost millions of pounds for no solid return, but there seemed no honourable alternative.

The British Consul to Abyssinia had been held prisoner for nearly three years by its barbaric and bibulous king. An envoy had been sent to offer a dignified protest and arrange the Consul's release, but he and his suite had also been clapped in chains, all of which made it clear that friendly negotiations were unlikely to achieve much.

None of this was tolerable by mid-Victorian standards. Private explorers (of whom there were many) took their lives in their own hands and could not always expect to be extricated from their self-made difficulties by the armed might of Britain, but persons in official positions, even the humblest, had the right to protection. An insult to an envoy was an insult to Queen Victoria herself and the code demanded retribution. Conciliation had failed, and force must now be used.

Unfortunately there was in this particular case a considerable possibility that force would fail—that by the time the expedition had reached its remote goal the king would have quietly cut the throats of his captives and retired even more deeply into the inaccessible depths of his vast territories. This was a chance

15

which had to be taken. One of the risks of empire was that from time to time its more remote servants came to unpleasant ends, a fact which was understood and accepted by the individuals concerned. They might not always be saved but it was presumably comforting for them to know that at least they would be avenged.

The army showed cautious enthusiasm for the operation; Britain's reputation as a military power had not altogether been enhanced in the Crimean War a few years before. Her soldiers had indeed fought, died, and eventually conquered in the Crimea despite the awful handicaps imposed on them by the administrative blunders of their superiors, but the ability to simply muddle through somehow was losing favour. By the mid-nineteenth century war was fast becoming a science, and sheer blind bull-dog courage of the old Albuera brand was no longer enough. Warfare had to be controlled by an effective staff and backed by an efficient administrative organization, and in these respects the British military machine had been found almost wholly wanting.

Events in the American Civil War, and even more recently the Austro-Prussian campaign of the previous year, had foreshadowed the pattern of modern war and had caused a great resurgence of interest in military affairs. The nations of Europe cast anxious, uneasy eyes on the preparations of their neighbours and began to reorganize their own armies on lines which the recent decisive Prussian victories had shown to be effective.

Great Britain had her own peculiar military problems created by her geographical position and her role as a great colonial power. She had always relied traditionally on the sea and the Royal Navy to protect her from invasion, while employing the bulk of her regular land forces overseas. But now the situation was beginning to change. The vast improvements in communications brought about by the railway, the steamship, and the telegraph had suddenly made it possible for a European enemy to concentrate strong forces with a speed and secrecy hitherto unknown, and might also make possible a quick dash across the Channel or the North Sea. The ditches had got narrower, and might need a great many more soldiers behind them as well as warships upon them. Reorganization and modernization were mandatory.

Much had already been done to reform the British Army since the Crimean debacle. By 1867, many of the improvements were well advanced and there may perhaps have been an understandable desire on the part of the military authorities to have a trial run somewhere, simply to make sure that the changes introduced had been along the right lines. The main object of the operation would be to test the staff and the administrative services. It could be taken for granted that the British soldier would fight; what had to be demonstrated was that he could also be fed and otherwise maintained under the most difficult circumstances likely to be encountered anywhere in the world. In this respect Abyssinia fitted the bill admirably.

There was, of course, no lack of eager volunteers to join the expedition. The British Army had seen comparatively little active service since the Mutiny and a great many officers, particularly the younger ones, were determined not to miss such a promising opportunity. Those selected regarded themselves as favoured mortals, nor did the steep rises in their insurance premiums do anything to lessen this view.

The press and the public naturally regarded the whole affair differently; to some it represented almost a crusade—a St George-like dash to rescue unhappy Britons from a dragon king; others regarded it sourly as likely to put a penny on the Income Tax. On the whole, the general feeling of the public was one of guarded pessimism—the events of the Crimea were too fresh in the minds of most for them to expect anything except failure in such a difficult task.

The correspondence columns of *The Times* were full of letters containing grave warnings of the horrid dangers likely to be encountered, together with much excellent advice on how these same dangers might be overcome. All that the bulk of the writers had in common (apart from supreme confidence in the rightness of their opinions) was the fact that few of them had any first hand experience of Abyssinia.

This was not surprising. Even now much of the country remains shrouded in mystery, and a hundred years ago it was true

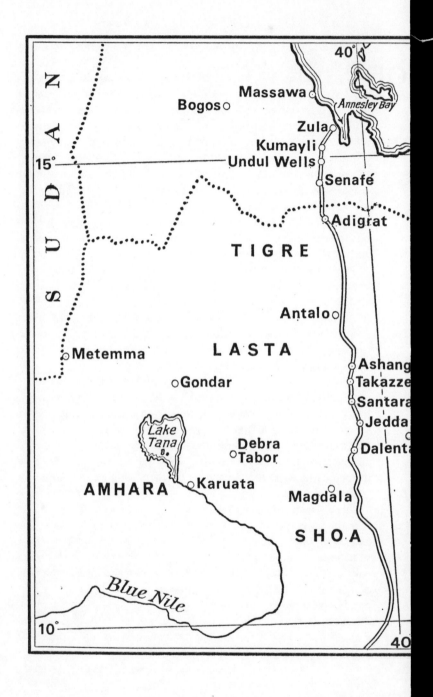

ORTHERN ABYSSINIA

R E D S E A

HOHO

YEMEN

ba Geshen

ALLA

ADEN

SOMALIA

45°

15°

10°

120   240 miles

H.J.B.

terra incognita, the legendary Ethiopia of Prester John. Only a few Europeans had ever visited it, and the mixture of fact and fable subsequently recorded by them had come to be regarded with a good deal of healthy scepticism. Perhaps the best known traveller was Bruce, a wandering Scot who had visited Gondar in 1770. Twenty years later he had published a record of his travels which had been received with the usual mixture of interest and incredulity then reserved for travellers' accounts of their wanderings in unknown places.

All that was known with any real certainty was that Abyssinia consisted mainly of a vast plateau, seamed by deep gorges and traversed by mountain ranges; a land of forests inhabited by wild beasts, and of fertile upland plains, all cut off from the rest of the world by a belt of inhospitable, waterless, salt desert; a land peopled by a warlike race akin to the Arabs, who professed a strange brand of Christianity and spoke a highly developed Semitic language with an alphabet and a literature—a people who ate raw meat and had a taste for almost constant internecine strife. It did not, at first sight, really provide the sort of detail on which to plan a major and highly complicated expedition.

* * *

Abyssinia had not always been isolated. The Greeks are said to have conquered much of the country in some remote period, although comparatively little is known of their sojourns save for a few ruins and one or two Greek sounding place names. Christianity came early. A philosopher sailing along the Red Sea coast in the third century, was caught and killed by the wild tribes inhabiting the littoral, but one of his nephews survived and eventually became a power at the court of the Abyssinian King. After some years he was allowed to return to Alexandria, where having recounted his adventures he was consecrated a Bishop and sent back to Abyssinia to convert the heathen. He was highly successful, and by the early years of the fourth century one of the oldest Christian churches in the world had been firmly established.

Early Abyssinian Christianity was particularly militant, and as soon as it had become well rooted in the country an overpowering desire arose to spread their creed in other lands. Peaceful penetration, the slow spread of the gospel by meek persistence, was not in the Abyssinian nature. Their first attempt at conversion was in the Yemen which they conquered bloodily with a view to the forcible imposition of their new religion on the people. At first they were successful, militarily at any rate, which made them an important power in the Middle East, and for some years they had an alliance with the Roman Empire. Various problems, mainly of communication, then rose which made it difficult for them to maintain their position in the Yemen. Its inhabitants showed a certain obstinate resistance to the joys of the new religion and an implacable hatred of the people attempting to impose it on them; in AD 590, they finally rebelled and drove out their oppressive missionary rulers.

This expulsion of the Abyssinian conquerors from Asia came just before the first rise of Islam. It is ironic that forty years after the Christian Abyssinians withdrew from Mecca, Mahomet was firmly established there, a prince, a prophet, and a conqueror, arrogantly summoning the Emperor of Greece and the Kings of Persia and Abyssinia to embrace *his* new religion, the true faith.

The rapid rise of Islam quickly isolated Abyssinia from the world; to the south and west of her were vast, unexplored tracts of tropical forest, and now the north and east were in the hands of the followers of the prophet, from whom no Christian could expect mercy. "Thereafter," wrote Gibbon, "Encompassed by the enemies of their religion, the Ethiopians slept for near a thousand years, forgetful of the world by whom they were forgotten."

The long isolation was first broken by the Portuguese who, by the fifteenth century, had become the explorers of the world, and in about 1490, one of them actually penetrated to the Abyssinian court where he was treated as an honoured guest and rose to high position. So popular was he, in fact, that he was never allowed to leave, but even in exile he never forgot his country. Eventually his influence caused the King to send an envoy to Portugal offering friendship, and in 1520 the Portuguese (who

21

at the time were conducting naval operations against the Turks in the Red Sea) took the opportunity of their close proximity to Abyssinia to send an embassy there. It was well received, and in the manner of the time stayed for seven years.

As the power of the Moslems waxed, so did their pressure against Abyssinia increase. By the time of the Portuguese embassy the situation had become sufficiently serious for the King to ask for help, and this the Portuguese were very ready to provide. Here was a vast, backward, but undoubtedly rich country, which needed only Portuguese initiative and development to set its stores of wealth flowing westwards. There was also the added attraction that its people were Christians; while assistance would undoubtedly develop trade, it could also be regarded as being in the nature of a crusade against the heathen—a happy blend of material and spiritual aims. It was true that their Christianity was of a strange and degenerate nature, but a few Jesuit priests could be trusted to restore orthodoxy quickly.

In 1541, the Portuguese despatched an expeditionary force from their settlements in Bombay, an example which was also to be followed by the British three hundred years later. It was commanded by a capable if somewhat arrogant young officer named de Gama (a brother of the Portuguese viceroy in India and a grandson of the great sailor and explorer Vasco de Gama) and consisted of four hundred and fifty musketeers and six light guns—a considerably more modest force than the one with which this book is mainly concerned.

The little army landed at Massawa, and having assembled sufficient mules to carry a few essentials it at once abandoned its communications and struck off southwards into the interior. After terrible hardships in the waterless desert along the coast, it succeeded in negotiating one of the rugged passes to the south and finally reached the main plateau where it was met by its Abyssinian allies. Here de Gama set about making various arrangements for a campaign which did not differ in essence from those made later by the British Army. Mules were obtained in large numbers, and great quantities of food and other essentials were assembled. The Portuguese even made rough carts—a form of transport completely unknown to the Abyssinians—and early in 1542, all being ready, they set off confidently to destroy the infidel.

The campaign, however, did not prosper. After some heartening initial successes, due in the main to the superior discipline and firepower of the small band of Portuguese, the joint force was severely defeated by a large and well-handled Moslem Army. De Gama himself was wounded and captured, and as he had previously made it something of a habit to send grossly insulting messages to the opposing general his fate was sealed. A formal offer to spare his life if he embraced Islam was met with a scornful refusal, after which his head was cut off—a swifter and more merciful end than he might perhaps have expected.

The fighting continued as it had done for hundreds of years, the surviving Portuguese playing a gallant part until casualties and disease finally eliminated them. After this no more soldiers were sent, but the opportunity offered by de Gama's entry into Abyssinian affairs was not lost, for a considerable number of Portuguese Jesuits entered the country and quickly set about establishing the *true* Christianity. They were not in the least conciliatory. They burned people for witchcraft and were generally violent and insolent; not unnaturally the Abyssinians disliked them intensely and much preferred their own local religion. The head of the mission eventually became so arrogant that he was exiled by the exasperated King, and thereafter the Jesuits' power waned; in about the middle of the seventeenth century the few survivors were conveniently disposed of by being handed over to the tender mercies of the Moslems, who in the meanwhile had occupied the Messawa coastal strip, thus sealing the hinterland off completely.

By the middle of the sixteenth century incursions into Abyssinian territory were also being made by the Gallas—a primitive but extremely fierce and warlike race. They probably originated in the area of what is now Somalia, but the fertile uplands of the plateau were much more attractive to them than their own sterile desert wastes. The Abyssinians resisted fiercely and with some success but little by little the interlopers gained ground, riding their hardy, surefooted ponies across the broken, mountainous country and fighting like wolves when attacked. By the eighteenth century they were in more or less firm occupation of a narrow, wedge-shaped piece of territory, pointing westwards along the approximate line of the twelfth parallel, and had practically cut Christian Abyssinia in two. At this time most of the Gallas were pagans, but a few later became Moslem.

Apart from almost continuous warfare against the Moslems and the Gallas, the Abyssinians were also involved in constant internal struggles. It was not practically possible to rule the country as an entity for, apart from the incursions of the Gallas, the great mountain ranges and the series of deep gorges split the country into a number of isolated and semi autonomous provinces. The rulers of these provinces regarded themselves as independent, and waged war against each other—and against the King—without scruple. Sometimes they combined briefly, either under the hand of an unusually strong monarch or the threat of a Moslem or Galla invasion, but in general the country was in a permanent state of internal strife, and its natural condition was anarchy. It was a predominantly feudal society in which the great bulk of the people, in spite of some injustice and oppression, had a strong and sincere attachment to their hereditary rulers. The country was primarily agricultural and pastoral; there was little trade, and as a consequence no middle class. Lower down the scale, slavery (although of a comparatively mild, domestic type) was common.

The great chiefs, secure in their isolation and comfortably conscious of the unswerving loyalty of their people, lived in a state of crude, barbaric splendour, gorged raw meat, drank considerable quantities of locally produced alcohol, and generally indulged themselves as their fancy dictated and their resources allowed. They were virtually independent and conducted the affairs of their provinces as they thought fit, without interference from the centre.

There was, of course, no penal code, such system as existed being based on customary law and enforced by flogging, mutilation, and death. The people seem nevertheless to have had clear rights, and it seems probable that the method ensured a rough and ready form of justice not unsuited to the Abyssinian character. Long isolation from the outside world, together with their naturally cruel natures and the almost unceasing warfare in which they indulged, had made them as fierce and savage as their Galla enemies, and such people were hardly likely to expect —or benefit from—too much kindness and leniency from those set over them.

The Abyssinians, rulers and ruled alike, were for the most part devout if militant Christians by their own strange standards (which amongst other things accepted animal sacrifices as a necessary part of the service of dedication of a new church and regarded it as natural that the liturgy should be enlivened by drumming and barbaric dancing). The country abounded in traces of the more liberal periods of its past, mainly in the form of great obelisks and other monuments, and many churches and monasteries—some of them very fine. But the long years of internal strife, particularly against the Gallas, had left the country far behind in cultural development.

It was perhaps natural in a land where only the priests (and by no means all of those) had any pretensions to literacy, that the bulk of its literature should consist of bible stories, devotional works, and homilies. A good deal of popular history also existed; most of it was drawn from the ancient chronicles and was surprisingly detailed, although, since much of it had been twisted in order to prove the descent of the Abyssinian people from Solomon, its accuracy was not always to be relied upon.

*   *   *

The position of the central monarchy, rarely very secure, was further weakened in the eighteenth century when a Christian king actually married a Galla woman in a desperate attempt to bring the two races together and end the hopeless, long-drawn-out struggle between them. The main effect of this effort was to infuriate the chiefs and set them against the king. The influence of the monarchy then quickly dwindled and subsequent rulers were little more than puppets in the hands of whichever of the great provincial chiefs happened to control them. The kings continued to be treated with the greatest respect and consideration, but their power had passed to other hands.

The first attempts by Britain to open any sort of official communication with Abyssinia came in the early nineteenth century when a Mr Salt, an official on the staff of the British Consul General in Egypt, was despatched to the country on a goodwill visit in 1810. His mission was not to the King, who lived in Gondar, a mere cypher, but to the court of the great prince who at that time was in effective control of much of the country north of the Galla wedge. It is perhaps typical of Abyssinian affairs at the time that the perplexed official had great difficulty in deciding which of several possible contenders for the role was most suitable. Having finally decided, however, he took with him two three-pounder field pieces and many other valuable presents, and was thus well received. Little came out of the visit except that it disposed the Abyssinians kindly toward Europeans and so facilitated the later entry of travellers into their country.

No further official contacts were made until 1841 when an officer of the Bombay Staff paid a visit, this time to the ruler of Shoa (who was for the time being in the ascendant). This officer also took with him a present of guns—articles which every Abyssinian ruler coveted—and was thus received kindly; from then on a small but steady stream of Europeans entered the country. The coastal strip was at that time held by the Turkish rulers of Egypt. The Turks were familiar with the might of Europe and took good care not to offend or hinder these various visitors.

As usual, among the first to arrive were missionaries; the Protestant Swiss Bishop Gobat visited Gondar in 1831 and returned again in 1835, this time with three missionaries. These remained in Adowa for three years but were then compelled to leave because of the prejudices of the local priests; they did not quit the country immediately, but spent some time in adventurous exploration. Others came too—naturalists, botanists, geologists, explorers, and engineers, together with a sprinkling of adventurers and soldiers of fortune. The various European revolutions which occurred in this period made it desirable for a number of people to leave their own countries post-haste, and to some of these Abyssinia offered a remote and reasonably anonymous refuge. The Roman Catholics, not deterred by the expulsion of their Protestant opposite numbers, also established themselves in fair numbers. Last, but perhaps not least, were various members of a London Society whose aim was to convert the Jews to Christianity; there were a considerable number of Jews in Abyssinia which thus appeared to offer them a fair field for their efforts.

In the mid-1870's two other persons arrived who were later destined to exert a powerful influence for good in the country. One of them, Plowden, was a young man of good family and education who had spent four years in a commercial firm in India before deciding that the life was not for him. On his way home he met one Bell, an ex-naval officer with a taste for adventure, and together they spent several years exploring Abyssinia, after which they took service under Ras Ali the *de facto* ruler of much of central and northern Abyssinia. They were honourable, intelligent young men, anxious only to carve careers for themselves and they served him well—so well in fact that in 1846 Ras Ali sent Plowden to England as an envoy, bearing gifts and friendly greetings to the Queen. In England, Plowden was able to impress upon the government the potential trading value of this largely unknown country, and Lord Palmerston appointed him British Consular agent at Massawa, with the particular task of encouraging and protecting British trade with the interior. Later Plowden was also appointed British Consul to Abyssinia, and dispatched back to Ras Ali with a wide variety of presents, and instructions to conclude a treaty of friendship and commerce if this could be arranged.

Plowden returned to Abyssinia in 1848 and made his way to the court of Ras Ali at Debra Tabor. The prince was delighted with the presents and readily signed a treaty. Communications within the country were so bad that there was little prospect of any immediate significant increase in trade, but the friendly atmosphere seemed to offer good auguries for the future. The ice had been broken and the sleeping giant offered the chance to emerge from its long isolation into the modern world of the nineteenth century. At the time it seemed probable that the chance would be taken. The initial traffic would have been one way since, although Europeans entered the country easily, few Abyssinians dared to leave it through the Turkish-held strip. Had trade prospects developed satisfactorily, however, there is no doubt that diplomatic pressure could quickly have compelled the Turks to display a more liberal attitude to the Abyssinians, who they held—without much justification—to be under their rule.

Plowden found on his return that Bell had married an Abyssinian woman of good family, and was happily settled in his adopted country. The two remained close friends and continued to exert a considerable influence for good in that part of the country ruled by Ras Ali.

CHAPTER 2
A Self Made Monarch

In 1818, a child was born in a remote, thickly forested valley near the Blue Nile and given the name of Kasa. His family had few claims to distinction. One of his uncles was a chief who had made a reputation for himself in the endless wars against the Gallas, but in general his parentage was modestly respectable rather than illustrious.

His father died when Kasa was very young leaving the family in such dire poverty that his mother was reduced to the humble role of market woman. The Abyssinians were fond of eating raw meat and this made them particularly susceptible to body worms. It was their custom to purge themselves once or twice a year. The draught they favoured was a nauseous but effective anthalmintic, made from the female flowers of the tree *Hagenia Abissinica* (which the locals called *Kosso*) and it was this potion that his mother sold to keep her family alive.

The boy survived and being an intelligent child his mother presently managed to get him into a monastery school to be educated as a scribe. Literacy was comparatively rare in Abyssinia, so that any man who could read or write could be reasonably sure of a dignified and profitable profession. Kasa learnt quickly and was soon not only able to read and write fluently but also well versed in Bible history and the psalms of David. He seemed to have found a respectable niche and could look forward to a moderately affluent future.

Fate then intervened in the shape of a turbulent chief who

decided to sack the monastery—it was the sort of thing which happened in Abyssinia. The young clerk survived this disaster and fled back to his own province, but he was no longer content with his chosen profession. He was an active and enterprising young man, and he soon became a soldier of fortune which— shorn of its glamorous associations—meant little more than bandit. It was a trade which at that time offered a great deal of scope, and although this new line of business was far removed from his old one he did well at it and began to prosper.

Kasa had a strong character and natural powers of leadership, which allied to his wild courage and his education, soon brought him to the fore. He became a leader in his own right and, as his reputation spread, his following increased rapidly until presently he commanded what was by local standards a large army.

There was no lack of opportunity in the country for a really enterprising soldier of his calibre and soon he had started on the career which was to bring him a throne. Amongst other enemies, he fought the Turkish-led Egyptians along the Northern frontier, and although beaten he learnt many lessons, among them the need for strict discipline and the value of well handled artillery.

At home he had better fortune; soon he was a power in the land and married the daughter of Ras Ali (which did not prevent him from leading a rebellion against his father-in-law a few years later). In this, as in other enterprises, he was also success- ful so that by 1854 Kasa was in more or less undisputed posses- sion of all the former dominions of Ras Ali. In the next year, having finally consolidated his position by the prompt elimin- ation of all possible rivals, he had himself crowned as King. The *Abuna* (the Patriarch of the Coptic Church in Abyssinia) did in fact protest mildly about this on technical grounds, but was sharply told that if he could not conduct the necessary services Kasa would become a Catholic, a threat which at once brought the *Abuna* to heel.

The young ruler had for long felt himself to be a man of destiny, and dreamed dreams of the eventual re-conquest of the whole non-Christian world. First he would subdue the Gallas; then he would convert the Moslem inhabitants of the country—

by forcible baptism if necessary; and finally, having consolidated his internal situation, he would lead a great crusade to expel the Turks from Jerusalem. His education and extensive reading of Abyssinian history had made him familiar with the legendary Theodore, the new Messiah of Solomon's line who would sooner or later arise to conquer the infidel. Kasa believed himself to be that man and had himself crowned as Theodore, by which name he was to be known henceforward.

His enemies laughed at Theodore's pretensions but the gesture had its effect. His steady success had attracted followers, as success will, and now his new identification with the legend brought more and more fighting men flocking to his standards. There was no real difficulty in proving his descent. A discreet word to the court genealogists made it clear what was required and soon he was in possession of a long and impeccable pedigree. The scribe turned bandit had done very well for himself.

He was, by any standards, a remarkable individual. At the time of his accession he was thirty-seven, a muscular, well built man with dark, but not negroid, features and piercing eyes. Long years of campaigning had made him proficient in the military arts. He was an excellent shot, an excellent spearman, a good athlete, and the best horseman in the country. He hated houses of all kinds and habitually lived in a tent. King Theodore was by Western standards completely untutored, but a man of high intelligence, with a particular interest in things mechanical. Under normal circumstances he was said to be generous and merciful but he had a quick, ungovernable temper which he had never found it necessary to curb, and in its grip he would do— or order done—things for which he was afterwards sorry. He was half-proud and half-resentful of his lowly parentage. His enemies had jibed at the fact that his mother had been a *Kosso* seller (not only a comparatively lowly occupation but one also associated with the sort of jokes seemingly inseparable from bowel functions). Theodore, knowing well enough who made these jokes, had the engaging habit of inviting them to feasts and proffering them large doses of kosso which they dared not refuse.

Possibly, Theodore's greatest single characteristic was his un-

31

swerving devotion to the Christian religion. His particular brand of Christianity was in many ways a fearsome one and European churchmen of all denominations were appalled at the things he did in its name; it is likely, however, that the Inquisition would have understood perfectly. In considering his nature and conduct, however, it is necessary to take into account both his lack of knowledge of the world beyond his borders and also the streak of unbridled savagery which appeared to be inseparable from the Abyssinian character.

He spent the first year of his reign in consolidating his position, and initially showed every sign of becoming an enlightened and progressive ruler. His first object—and one which is common to all men in his position—was to break the power of any possible rivals, which he did by placing the government of the various provinces under trusted henchmen. He also abolished slavery (on paper anyway, although in practice it apparently continued to flourish), reduced customs dues, and placed his soldiers under strict discipline in order to prevent their plundering the local inhabitants. All this made him popular with his subjects and appeared to be establishing the foundations of what the country most required—a period of just rule under a strong monarch.

Plowden made his way to the court as soon as he heard of Theodore's accession and there found Bell, who had already offered his services to the new ruler. Both these two had a great effect, for Theodore trusted them and valued their advice and assistance, and under their tactful guidance could sometimes be persuaded to temper his natural impetuosity and behave with circumspection. Their joint efforts were warmly seconded by the Queen, an intelligent and enlightened woman who constantly preached restraint and moderation and who provided by her own example an influence often able to curb the worst excesses of his sudden, violent rages.

Initially, therefore, all seemed well; Theodore had established himself swiftly and firmly on the throne and had he been content to rule only the two great northern provinces of Tigré and Amhara his prospects would have been bright. In time he might even have gradually extended his influence to the whole country and so given it the moderate, stable government which it badly needed.

Patience and moderation, however, were not in his nature, and his passionate, militant Christianity could not be suppressed. As soon as he was well established, Theodore started military operations against the Gallas to the south of him, and being a capable soldier with a brave and loyal army quickly achieved a considerable measure of success. The Gallas, not being Christians, were unworthy of mercy and he slaughtered them in horrifying numbers until even those brave savages were temporarily dismayed and withdrew to their various remote mountain strongholds to be out of his reach. They could wait. Previous conquerors had always retired sooner or later to their own country. But now Theodore came to an important decision. He would not withdraw, but would establish his own permanent headquarters in some strong place deep in Galla territory in order to keep them under his eye. They were subdued for the moment but he knew enough of their nature to be sure that sooner or later they would need another sharp reminder that his hand was heavy. The site he chose was a rugged rock bastion known as an *Amba*. The country was scattered with such places and they played much the same role in Abyssinia that the castles of the feudal barons had done in mediaeval Europe. The particular *Amba* selected by Theodore for his fortress was called Magdala.

He established a garrison there and went on to conquer Shoa, the large province lying below the Galla wedge; this did not take long, for his reputation had preceded him and the opposition melted away at his approach. He was soon on his way back to Magdala, carrying amongst his trophies the guns presented to the Prince of Shoa by the British in 1841. He also seized Menelik, the heir to Shoa, and carried him off as a hostage.

While Theodore was engaged in these operations trouble broke out behind him in his own northern provinces. A rebel chief had seized power in Tigré, apparently with some discreet support from the French Catholic mission, and there was a good deal of intermittent fighting going on between the rebels and his own loyal supporters. During a lull in the fighting Plowden decided that the time had come to visit his consulate at Massawa. He set out in 1860, but had the misfortune to fall in with a wandering band of rebels under a minor chief and was seriously wounded in the fight which ensued. Theodore was too far away to intervene militarily but when he heard that Plowden was in rebel hands he at once offered a large ransom for his release. This was accepted and Plowden was handed over, but died from his wounds a few days later.

Theodore became very angry, which always boded ill for someone. He decided to deal with the matter personally and soon ran the chief and his band to ground. The fight that followed was brief and bitter, for although the rebels were outnumbered they knew they could expect no mercy. Bell, who was with Theodore, actually killed the rebel chief with his own hand, but was himself then shot down. Theodore, enraged at the death of the second of his closest friends, lost all control and ordered the slaughter of every rebel that could be found. Upwards of fifteen hundred died in this way, including the brother of the rebel chief—he was captured and brought in a prisoner and Theodore cut him down with his own hand.

Theodore then set out for Tigré to deal with the main rising there, and this too was easily accomplished for the rebels broke and ran at the mere rumour of his advance. The rebel chief and his brother both fled, but there was no shelter for them in Tigré and they were soon captured. Theodore wasted no time with them, but cut one hand and one foot off each and left them tied up in the sun without food, water, or shade. The brother succumbed quickly, but the chief himself had plenty of time to repent his misdeeds, for it took him three full days to die.

Theodore's Queen died about this time and the sudden loss of his three most trusted advisers led to a rapid deterioration of his character. He had previously had the benefit of much honest and disinterested advice but this was suddenly cut off; now he was surrounded by flattering and calculating courtiers anxious to influence him for their own ends. He was by then firmly in control of the country again but he seemed to have developed a taste for blood. He had always loved the excitement of battle but now he appeared to enjoy killing for its own sake and soon launched another campaign against the luckless Gallas with the evident object of exterminating them. Villages were burnt, often with the inhabitants inside them; fields laid waste, and women and children sold ruthlessly into slavery to his enemies, the Egyptians. The few warriors who survived were savagely mutilated so that they could neither fight nor reproduce. The whole country reeked of blood and death.

After this campaign Theodore married again for political reasons but the union was not a success. His Queen, whose family he had maltreated, hated him and after bearing a son had left him. This caused a further deterioration in his character. He started drinking heavily and although previously a continent man also began to associate with a variety of concubines, chief of whom—strangely enough—was a fat, voluptuous Galla woman. His bouts of temper became more frequent, and the effects of alcohol rendered them more dangerous; when in their grip he would order the most terrible atrocities, none daring to oppose him. Deserters were branded and mutilated, and traitors (or suspected traitors), had stakes driven through their hearts. There were no trials. An angry word, a drunken whim, and people were flogged, flayed, shot, stabbed, or merely flung alive over some convenient precipice to die in their own good time. The discipline of his considerable army of soldiers grew lax and their plundering and insolent behaviour further oppressed the civilian population. All his earlier resolutions were forgotten. He had to a great extent reverted to the traditional savage Abyssinian chief, although on rather a larger scale than was usual. 1764525

Discontent was widespread and plotting began against him. For the moment his reputation protected him, but many people were only waiting for a chance to pull him down. In his more rational moments Theodore continued to plan for the great moment when he would be strong enough to sweep the Turks into the sea and place the holy city of Jerusalem once more under Christian dominion. He was well aware of the need for modern methods and modern weapons if he were to achieve this, and he thus encouraged the entry into the country of European engineers, artisans, and skilled technicians to provide him with the equipment he needed. Extensive cannon foundries were set up and guns and mortars of considerable size were cast. Powder mills were also established and Greek and Armenian merchants acted as his agents in the purchase of muskets from various sources in Europe.

Theodore was shrewd enough to realize that only liberal treatment would induce competent European workmen to serve him and he therefore paid his employees well and treated them with every consideration. Some brought their wives with them, others married either Abyssinian women or the half-caste progeny of one or two earlier mixed marriages. Soon there was a small predominantly European community in the country but they had the good sense to steer clear of internal intrigues and confine themselves to their families and their manufactures. Loyalty and hard work were all that Theodore asked for and when given these he in his turn could be kind and generous.

A Protestant mission decided shrewdly to send out a team of skilled artisans who were also lay preachers, and soon a party of six workmen of generally superior character arrived. Theodore accepted them gladly and set them to work casting ordnance and making roads, but they were given no encouragement— indeed no opportunity—to preach; Theodore needed technical rather than spiritual guidance and made this clear to them from the start.

A number of other missionaries (including one to convert the Jews) also established themselves. The Abyssinians, who considered their own brand of Christianity superior to any other, were not converted in significant numbers, but tolerated the missionaries' presence for the sake of good European relations generally. Other, more materially minded individuals, also drifted in—Germans, Austrians, Swiss, Poles, and Russians—mostly ex-soldiers or simple adventurers seeking positions under the warlike king. One of the few Englishmen to take service with Theodore was a certain Charles Speedy. He had served for several years as an officer in the British and Indian armies but had resigned with the intention of settling in New Zealand. *En route*, Speedy visited Abyssinia and after a prolonged elephant shooting and general exploring trip he spent some time at Theodore's camp and accompanied him on some of his endless military expeditions. Speedy apparently held an independent military command under Theodore for some time and established a reputation for great courage. He was physically a giant —some six feet five inches in height and endowed with enormous strength. (One of the accomplishments which endeared him to Theodore was his ability to cut the carcase of a sheep in two lengthwise with a single blow of a sabre—a feat which no Abyssinian ever succeeded in emulating.) Speedy later acted as vice-consul in Massawa for a while, but soon got bored and left to continue his journey to New Zealand early in 1864.

*   *   *

When the news of Plowden's death reached England, a new consul was at once nominated. The choice fell on Captain Charles Duncan Cameron, and this appointment set in train a sequence of events which was to end with a single pistol shot in the *Amba* of Magdala some six years later.

Cameron was a type of Englishman found fairly frequently in the nineteenth century, an accomplished linguist and a man of adventurous and restless disposition, with a preference for the wilder places of the world. He was the son of a Colonel in the Buffs and had himself started his career as a subaltern in the 45th Regiment. Cameron went with them to South Africa but resigned in 1851 after service in the Kaffir war. Thereafter, he had for a time been a magistrate in Natal and a leader of native irregulars in the War of 1852–3. He returned to the Army for the Crimean War and saw service in Turkey. When it was over he joined the consular service and after various Middle Eastern postings arrived in Massawa in 1862.

His instructions from the British Government were clear and unequivocal—he was to base himself at Massawa and be careful to avoid becoming involved in any factional disputes in the country. Moreover, he was ordered to go in person to Theodore and present him with a handsome rifle and a pair of fine pistols, together with a letter from Queen Victoria expressing her gratitude for the efforts he had made to save Plowden.

37

The new consul reached the court in October and was well received by Theodore who expressed his pleasure at the gifts and remarked that he was very grateful for the Queen's good wishes, adding casually that he had slaughtered some fifteen hundred men in order to demonstrate his feelings for her. The King's main preoccupation was still with the Moslem menace, and he spoke constantly of plans to drive them away from his borders and so open up the country to European influence.

Cameron was dismissed after a month at court with a letter to Queen Victoria, in which Theodore expressed his thanks, reiterated that he had slaughtered rebels by the hundred in order to avenge Plowden's death and so gain her friendship, and also made frequent references to the evils and oppressions of the Turks. He wrote that he proposed to send an Embassy to England, presumably with the object of obtaining military assistance, and ended his letter with the phrase "see how Islam oppresses the Christian".

At the same time he sent a similar letter to France, perhaps with some shadowy idea of playing one country off against the other. This letter was carried by a Frenchman, one Bardel, a wandering ex-soldier who had for a time been servant to Cameron.

The letter to the Queen reached the Foreign Office via Aden early in 1863 and appears to have caused some embarrassment there. Christianity was of course highly esteemed by the pious Victorians but they could not afford to take too narrow a view of religious matters. They ruled a large Empire which included people of all races and religions, and although no doubt in theory they would have been delighted to see them all united in the true faith, in practice they had to be very careful. The terrible example of India was still before their eyes. Only four years previously much of the great sub-continent, which included among its peoples some millions of Moslems, had been set ablaze by a military mutiny which had at least some of its causes in religious matters. They could thus hardly be expected to view with enthusiasm any suggestion that they should join an obscure monarch—Christian though he might be—in a crusade against Islam.

After some anxious debate a course of masterly inactivity was decided on. This fellow Theodore was, after all, a relatively unimportant ruler, and by all accounts his interpretation of Christianity was a strange one. If nothing at all were done—so ran the comforting theory—he might perhaps forget all about it and busy himself with the numerous internal problems which beset him. The letter was therefore laid aside and no reply sent.

*　　*　　*

Cameron did not return direct to Massawa, but travelled round the northern frontiers of the country. The Egyptian lands bordering Abyssinia produced cotton in considerable quantities and the Foreign Office had instructed him to investigate the possibility of obtaining new supplies there. Previously, the southern states of America had been the principal growers but the American Civil War had cut off supplies from that source; cotton operatives were starving in Lancashire, and trade was almost at a standstill. It was imperative to get the raw material from somewhere, and very understandable that the Government should wish to take all possible steps to keep the industry going.

During this journey Cameron also visited Bogos, a small area where the Abyssinians were continually raided by the Egyptians. For some reason in the past the British had exerted themselves to protect these particular individuals, and Cameron in this respect was simply continuing the policy of his predecessors. At the end of his trip he was taken ill, and decided that rather than return to the unhealthy climate of Massawa, he would move to the more temperate climate of the highlands to recuperate. In any case he was expecting a reply to Theodore's letter and wished to be at the court when it arrived so that he might deliver it personally to the King.

Meanwhile, the French had also posted a consul to Abyssinia. The French consul arrived in company with another wandering Englishman, Henry Dufton, who had spent some years travelling in Abyssinia. At first the Frenchman was well received, but presently Bardel returned from France; with some lack of tact the authorities in Paris had not considered him a suitable emissary and had sent back the letter unopened, upon which Theodore at once expelled the consul. Cameron, who was waiting at Gondar for a reply to his letter, must have regarded this as a piece of diplomatic luck.

Soon after the expulsion of the French consul Theodore for the first time laid violent hands on a European. One of the missionaries, Stern, had been unwise enough to write a long letter to his society in which he criticized Theodore freely, raised the old chestnut of his mother being a *Kosso* seller and stated that in his opinion the slaughter of the rebels after the death of Plowden and Bell had been murder pure and simple. Even more unwisely the society had the letter printed as a pamphlet and circulated it widely. Stern became worried and confided in Bardel. He could not have made a worse choice, for Bardel went at once to Theodore. Stern's baggage was searched and copies of the offending pamphlet found, and he and his associate Rosenthal were at once put in chains. Cameron was not really worried by this. He considered, very reasonably, that Theodore had some grounds for being angry, and that the missionaries would be released when his wrath had cooled.

In 1864, a young Irishman named Kerens, who acted as Cameron's secretary, arrived back with the long awaited dispatches. They contained no reply to Theodore's letter—only a brief and peremptory instruction to Cameron to return at once to Massawa and not to meddle with matters which did not concern him. The lack of a reply could not be concealed from Theodore, and with much justification he regarded the omission as a deliberate personal insult.

Theodore had begun to suspect the good faith of the British Government some time before. The first intimation came from Jerusalem. The British, in a casual but kind-hearted way, had at one time used their good offices to ensure fair treatment for Abyssinian pilgrims to the various shrines, but eventually the Turkish rulers of the country had declared arbitrarily that all Abyssinians were Turkish subjects, and thereafter rejected all British representations on the subject. The British, who in fact had no rights in the matter, accepted this mildly, but Theodore regarded it as an abject surrender to Islam and resented it bitterly. Even more suspect had been Cameron's visit to the neigh-bouring Egyptian provinces the year before. No one had ever bothered to explain the cotton situation to Theodore and as far as he was concerned the British were consorting with his bitter enemies.

The concept of constitutional monarchy was of course far outside Theodore's understanding. He was an absolute monarch himself and he naturally could not conceive of any other kind. This being so, he considered that he had been personally insulted by Queen Victoria who had ignored his offers of friendship and was apparently negotiating with his enemies. His reactions were simple and direct. Cameron and the three other Europeans of his suite were sent to the great fortress of Magdala and placed in irons.

Theodore now had six European prisoners, and having taken the initial step of confining them he did not thereafter scruple to ill-treat them. The missionaries were tortured systematically in order to make them confess their wrongness in the matter of the book; Cameron underwent the same treatment although in his case there was no apparent motive save malice. He was regularly subjected to a form of primitive rack in which twenty strong men hauled on ropes attached to his limbs until he fainted; he was also flogged with a hippopotamus hide whip until he bled freely and then rolled in dry sand. At all times the prisoners were kept closely chained and fed on bread and water, with no apparent prospect of release, or even relaxation of the severity of their treatment. Indeed their real fear was that things, bad as they were, would get worse. Theodore, although always perfectly rational, was becoming more and more subject to fits of mad rage in which his only desire seemed to be for blood. When Menelik (the heir to Shoa) escaped, the European prisoners thought their last hour had come. Theodore actually watched with his glass as the fugitive crossed the ravine, and saw him greeted by the Gallas to whom he had fled. Then he sent for all his Galla prisoners (numbering several hundreds) and having had their hands and feet cut off flung them over a precipice to die. Cameron and the others fully expected the same treatment, but Theodore, having expended the worst of his rage on the

41

unfortunate Gallas, contented himself with chaining them wrist to ankle.

Their only ray of hope was that a chief, a member of Theodore's household with whom Cameron had previously been on friendly terms, undertook (for a consideration) to get messages to Massawa. Cameron had of course no way of ensuring that the offer was genuine in the first place, but his doubts were soon put at rest when a reply to his first letter was received from the Political Resident at Aden. Thereafter this tenuous chain of communication remained in effective being as long as it was needed.

CHAPTER 3
An Envoy in Chains

THE news of Cameron's imprisonment created something of a sensation in England. The British were very conscious of their role as rulers of a great Empire, and this sort of behaviour by a petty African potentate was looked upon as a gratuitous insult. The real problem was to decide what action should be taken. This was no local, easily accessible ruler, to be overawed by a gunboat or the move of a couple of battalions to his frontiers. Effective military action against this particular offender was likely to be both difficult and extremely expensive.

Thanks to the good offices of the friendly chief, Cameron was in fairly regular communication with civilization. The system was naturally slow, since letters were carried by messengers, but few if any went astray. The bearers were paid twenty Maria Theresa dollars for each missive delivered, and as this involved a round trip of nearly eight hundred miles, it was a cheap enough price.

After the departure of Captain Speedy there was no permanent British representative at Massawa, so all messages from Cameron went to Colonel Merewether of the Bombay Staff Corps, at that time Political Resident in Aden. Matters could not have been handled by a better man. Merewether was an experienced soldier who, after service in a Native Infantry Regiment, had spent some years in the Scinde Irregular Horse under the famous Colonel Jacob from whom he had learnt to combine active soldiering with diplomacy and administration. He had seen service at the second siege of Multan and during the Mutiny had commanded the Baluchi frontier area, a thankless, arduous, task which he had discharged skilfully. Merewether had been in Aden since 1863 and had quickly established a reputation for both firmness and fairness. He favoured conciliation, but when this failed he was quite ready to resort to sharp punitive measures. He was an active, intelligent, and energetic officer who enjoyed arduous duty, and he at once set about making arrangements for the comfort and eventual release of Cameron.

At first all he could do was to keep the consul well supplied with money, and to try and keep up his spirits with cheerful, hopeful messages. Cameron was by then under no illusions as to the seriousness of his situation, and in a letter of February 1864, made it clear that in his opinion he could not hope for freedom until Theodore's original cause for complaint had been dealt with and a reply sent to his message. The Government chose to ignore this too, but Cameron's letter found its way into *The Times* and other papers, and at once there was an uproar in Parliament and the Country generally. The Government took heed of this public outcry and eventually decided to send a reply to Theodore in a belated attempt to conciliate him and obtain the release of his captives. After some deliberation it was decided that the letter should be carried by Mr Hormuzd Rassam, Colonel Merewether's first assistant in Aden.

The choice was in many ways a strange one. Rassam was a Chaldean Christian from Mosul in Mesopotamia. He was a man of good intelligence and education, and had attended an English university, after which he had spent many years in the service of Layard, the well-known archaeologist, whose work lay mainly in the Middle East. When Layard, a man of great influence, had finally returned to England he had been able to arrange Rassam's appointment to the moderately lucrative and not too arduous political post in Aden—a somewhat unlikely preparation for the unusual mission with which he was now entrusted.

Rassam's terms of reference were vague; he was to conciliate Theodore and try to obtain the release of the prisoners by persuasion. No demands were to be made. Rassam (and Dr Blanc of the Bombay Medical Service who accompanied him in a professional capacity) arrived in Massawa in July 1864, and Rassam's first action was to establish contact with Theodore and try to obtain his formal permission to enter the country. There was however much delay. Communication was slow and Theodore's whereabouts vague; a great deal of time passed without anything much happening. In the same period public apprehension was kept alive by the stream of more or less despairing messages which continued to reach England from Cameron.

The matter was raised repeatedly in Parliament during the sessions of 1865. The Government made some efforts to smother discussions on the grounds that, as Theodore was said to have the English papers read to him regularly, he was likely to take grave exception to some of the full-blooded epithets bestowed on him by indignant members during debates on the subject.

The feeling that Rassam was unsuitable as an envoy also gained ground. It was said that a senior officer of one of the Armed Services would carry more weight with a soldier of Theodore's reputation than would this rather mild political gentleman. In an effort to compromise, a third member, Lieutenant Prideaux of the Bombay Staff Corps and Merewether's third assistant in Aden, was added to the party.

It is difficult not to feel that a senior soldier or sailor accustomed to authority would have made a more suitable envoy. Theodore considered himself first and foremost a soldier, and might perhaps have been flattered by the visit of someone with a distinguished fighting record. In fairness it must perhaps also be said that it was difficult to decide how a man of Theodore's mentality would react to anyone or anything.

By the middle of 1865, anti-Rassam feeling had become so strong in political and other circles that the Government again bowed to public opinion and sent a message of recall to Massawa where Rassam was still waiting for Theodore's permission to proceed. In his place they appointed, not a distinguished service officer but Mr W. G. Palgrave, a noted Arabist and explorer, who at once departed for Egypt laden with presents and conciliatory letters for the erring monarch.

Rassam chose to ignore the letter of recall. Instead he went to Egypt, where he telegraphed the Government that Cameron had been released. He also made it clear that this improvement in the situation was due entirely to his own tact and diplomacy and insisted that he and no one else should go to Abyssinia.

There was a brief tussle over this at home, but if Rassam had detractors he also had powerful friends in high places, for it was soon decreed that in view of the improvement in the situation he should proceed as originally arranged. At this stage his hand was much strengthened by the receipt of a letter from Theodore which although ungracious in tone was not actually hostile. Rassam, therefore, took over the various gifts from Palgrave and departed again for Aden, leaving his rival sitting angrily but helplessly in Egypt. It soon transpired that there was no truth in the tale of Cameron's release, and although Rassam later explained that he meant released *from chains* his explanation sounded lame.

When Rassam arrived at Aden, Colonel Merewether at once sent him on to Massawa with orders to leave for the interior immediately. His trust in his deputy cannot have been absolute, since he went so far as to request the master of the ship on which the envoy travelled, to ensure as far as he was able, that Rassam did not linger in Massawa longer than was absolutely necessary.

Rassam, having finally started, then decided to make a wide circuit round the northern frontiers of Abyssinia and enter via Metemma; his reasons for this are not clear unless it was because Theodore was believed to be in Gondar at that time. A second letter then arrived from the King and this time its tone was a good deal more hopeful. Not only would Theodore be pleased to receive the envoy, but would actually send three senior officials from his own household to meet the party and make all the subsequent arrangements for them to reach his court. Rassam was much cheered by the message. Although it is unfair to judge him harshly on too little evidence there is some indication that he was seriously unnerved by the whole business. Nor is it easy to blame him. His whole previous experience appears to have been in relatively minor administrative posts where adherence to routine, a certain smoothness of manner, and an apparent anxiety to please were the prime requisites for success.

He was clearly not a man of decisive action or commanding character, and the prospect of bearding a half-mad monarch with the sort of reputation which Theodore enjoyed, and then requesting the return of Cameron and the other prisoners in the name of a Queen to whom he himself can have owed little allegiance, must have appalled him. Nevertheless there was much to hope for too, for the man who successfully negotiated the release of the prisoners would achieve fame and might expect considerable rewards. Rassam made the necessary arrangements, and he and his party started for the interior.

They met their Abyssinian escorts at the place agreed and thereafter everything went smoothly, but very slowly. Carriers and pack animals had to be engaged, but as these would not leave their own area they had to be discharged at every provincial boundary and a new set engaged and organized—a frustrating and time wasting business for the envoy and his companions but not one which worried the Abyssinians. Prideaux noted with some surprise that Theodore was little more than a name in many places, and that their guides trusted as much to their own feudal claims to service as to the threat of Theodore's authority.

They were received with great pomp at Theodore's court and after a short rest they unpacked their best uniforms and rode off in state on gaily caprisoned mules to meet the King, who greeted them affably and treated them as honoured guests. He accepted their presents from the Queen gracefully, and although he then launched into a long and involved tirade against Cameron he did eventually say that he would release the prisoners. His behaviour throughout was perfectly rational and Rassam and his companions began to think that perhaps he had been misjudged.

A day or two later the King—always of a restless disposition —decided to move his camp to the western shores of Lake Tana, and the whole unwieldy caravan, fighting men, servants, women, children, mules, horses, and camels crawled off eastwards, the unruly soldiers eating up the country as they went. The mission moved with them and the King continued to show its members every consideration. He appeared to be particularly fond of Rassam and spent long hours riding beside him, discussing a host of subjects with him. He also insisted on pressing considerable sums of money on him as expenses for his journey, brushing aside Rassam's protestations that all had been well provided for by the Queen of England whose representative he was. Altogether, Theodore gave him fifteen thousand Maria Theresa dollars, which required seven or eight mules to carry them. Waldemeier, one of the artisan lay-preachers, had a close (if understandably precarious) friendship with the King, and afterwards wrote that at the time, Theodore was under the firm impression that Rassam had come not as a visitor to negotiate the release of the prisoners only, but as a permanent ambassador; this may well be true.

When they reached the site of the new encampment at Lake Tana, Theodore sent the mission on to Kuarata with repeated assurances that the prisoners would be freed as soon as possible and sent on to them. He also ordered his artisans to go with the party so that they would not lack European companionship during their stay there.

On 12th March the prisoners from Magdala were escorted into Kuarata to the great joy of the mission, which must have felt that its task was almost completed. A few days later a letter from Theodore arrived asking Rassam to write to Queen Victoria and request her to send him a number of engineers and workmen. Rassam however, still a little distrustful, demurred at this suggestion and replied that it would be very much better if he were to go to England personally in order to explain Theodore's needs in detail to the Queen. The prisoners in the meanwhile, although still under discreet surveillance, were allowed a great deal of personal freedom and were able to ride about the countryside as they pleased. They were also allowed their firearms and permitted to go on shooting expeditions. On receipt of Rassam's reply Theodore sent for him and harangued him on the subject of technical assistance in developing his country. Rassam still temporized and the King, although apparently extremely angry, sent him off back to Kuarata with still more promises of freedom.

On 13th April Cameron and his party were actually sent off, ostensibly towards Massawa, while Rassam and his companions

1   A view of Annesley Bay as it is today, with the remains of one of the stone piers. It speaks well of the skill of the original Indian Engineers who built these piers, over a hundred years ago. (*Stephen Bell & John Fynn*)

2   The base camp at Zula, a few weeks after the landing. Part of the light railway may be seen to the left of the photograph. (*National Army Museum*)

3 The mule lines at Zula. These animals were to prove one of the biggest problems during the early days of the expedition—'but soon they began to die and presently the desert for miles around the base was littered with swollen carcases.' (*National Army Museum*)

4–5 A panoramic view of the shipping in Annesley Bay. Some idea may be gained from this picture of the vast quantities of men and material required for even a relatively small expedition. *(National Army Museum)*

6   General Napier with officers of the Royal Engineers. These
excellent photographs were taken by a specially detailed unit of
the Royal Engineers, and show surprising quality for their age.
(Army Museums Ogilby Trust)

7   No. 3 Battery, 21st Brigade Royal Artillery, commanded by
Captain (Brevet Lt-Colonel) L. W. Penn. *(Army Museums Ogilby
Trust)*

8   Captain Fellowes, RN, with the Naval Brigade at Guna-guna.
The Naval Brigade proved to be one of the most efficient units
in the expedition; they very soon acquired an affinity with their
pack animals and made excellent muleteers. *(Army Museums
Ogilby Trust)*

9 The 27th Bombay Native Infantry (1st Baluchis), under the command of Major H. Beville. (*Army Museums Ogilby Trust*)

were called back to the Royal camp in order to make their formal farewells to Theodore, after which they were to rejoin Cameron by a different route round the lake.

When they arrived at the camp they were treated with the usual courtesy and ceremony and presently escorted to the King's tent. Theodore himself was not present, but most of his principal chiefs were assembled there. Once inside, the situation changed swiftly, and they were seized unceremoniously and publicly searched, their arms and some of their other personal effects being removed. They were then confined under guard in a small tent, pitched in the full heat of the sun, for two days. At the end of this time the dejected Cameron and his people were also brought back under heavy escort and confined nearby, although the two groups were not at that stage permitted to communicate with each other.

On 17th April Theodore had all his captives brought before him and harangued them at great length on his need of machinery and European workmen to operate it. He then dictated a personal letter to Queen Victoria and also ordered Rassam to write a second one to the Secretary of State. Both of these letters reiterated his need for engineers, workmen, and machinery, particularly for making arms and munitions, and now he also demanded artillery instructors to train his own gunners.

These letters were sent off with Mr Flad, another of the artisan lay-preachers whom Theodore liked and trusted (although Flad's European wife remained in the camp as a hostage against his safe return). Flad left the camp on 21st April and was in London by 10th July. Apart from the two official letters, he carried with him a number of private messages from the prisoners to their relatives, all of which spoke of the considerate treatment they were receiving. It was generally supposed that Rassam had persuaded them to do this so that if any of their letters appeared in the English press Theodore would not be offended. This may or may not be true. What is certain is that in spite of all their assurances the prisoners were heavily loaded with chains long before Flad reached London, the only exception being Rassam, whom Theodore treated with a great deal of consideration throughout.

Cholera then broke out round Lake Tana and Theodore again moved his camp, this time to Debra Tabor, while the prisoners were sent off to the fortress of Magdala. They travelled during the rains, in great haste and extreme discomfort, and when they finally reached their destination they were once again loaded with chains. This fortunately was only temporary and their situation soon improved. Theodore was hated by a great many of his own people so that their jailers, once away from his immediate influence, were prepared to allow some relaxation—for a consideration.

Fortunately Cameron had already established a reliable chain of communication, so that messengers got through to the coast fairly regularly and returned with considerable sums of money, always in the bulky Maria Theresa dollars, and a variety of other luxuries to ease their lot. All arrangements at the other end were made by the energetic Colonel Merewether, but in the last resort the whole scheme depended on the honesty and reliability of the Abyssinian messengers and it is a remarkable fact that none of the money or other goods ever appear to have gone astray. The arrival of cash in large quantities made an immediate difference to their condition. Their chains were removed, they were allowed servants, and much of their property was restored to them. They were also allotted houses and plots of land and, as Merewether sent supplies of vegetable seeds, they were able to cultivate gardens which gave them an interest and also enabled them to vary their diet. There was no shortage of local food and drink, so that all in all their material condition was very much improved. Cameron was their main worry, since his earlier ill-treatment had left him a very sick man. Blanc did all he could for him but the main thing Cameron needed was freedom and security and this was denied to them all. However improved their condition might be they were still captives, still at the whim of the strange unbalanced monarch who had imprisoned them.

*   *   *

In the meanwhile Theodore remained in the area of Debra Tabor, and although it was the only part of Abyssinia which remained in any sense faithful to him he treated it, and allowed his soldiers to treat it, in a most cruel and oppressive manner. He pillaged Gondar and burned most of the town—even the churches had their treasures carried away by the Christian King. The citizenry was slaughtered by the hundred for no apparent reason; even Theodore's wild soldiers were appalled and deserted in steadily increasing numbers. It could not last for ever, and by the beginning of 1867 the whole country was in a state of general, although largely unco-ordinated, rebellion. Theodore was no more than nominal ruler of even this small area. His actual domain extended no further than the range of his guns— always excepting his last great fortress of Magdala.

In April the people of Debra Tabor, terrified by Theodore's oppression, attempted to court favour by offering to have cast for him a huge mortar, larger than anything then in his battery. The offer was at once accepted, for Theodore had great faith in the power of cannon—the larger the better.

The technical side of the operation was carried out by the King's favourite artisan, the versatile Waldemeier, and the enormous task of making moulds and building furnaces to melt the vast quantities of brass required, began almost at once. Waldemeier, uneasily conscious that his present favour with the King was unlikely to survive a failure, spent the long period of preparation in a state of extreme apprehension. Nor were his worries reduced by the fact that Theodore, fascinated by all technical or mechanical processes, was in more or less constant attendance at the foundry.

The great day came when the piece was cast. Fortunately for all concerned it was a success, and Theodore spent hours gloating over his new possession with its squat barrel and enormous twenty-one inch bore. He had heard enough of the Crimean war to know the part played by siege guns and he christened his new mortar, "Sebastopol". His country might be slipping from his grasp but he did not appear to care. In his simple creed artillery meant power, and as long as he remained in possession of his great guns he remained a great man.

His artillery could do nothing for him in Debra Tabor. His army had practically eaten up the countryside and the little that was left was either hidden or even destroyed by the desperate peasants to prevent it falling into the King's hands. Famine now threatened, and the atmosphere of his camp was foul with the stench of the unburied carcases of horses, mules, and camels which had died from starvation. At this period even the artisans became desperate and hatched a plot to escape, but unfortunately confided in Bardel, the King's French jackal, who at once reported the matter to Theodore. They were immediately imprisoned, and for a long time a hideous death by mutilation faced them. Theodore then changed his mind and simply left them in chains. He was considering a move, a very long and difficult move, and the technical problems of transporting his artillery could not be solved without their superior knowledge.

CHAPTER 4

Force Decided On

THE news that Rassam and his companions had joined
Cameron and the others in captivity made it clear that there was
little more to be gained by diplomacy. As soon as Colonel
Merewether heard of this latest development he hurried to Massawa to meet Flad who was on his way there with the letters
to Queen Victoria and the British Government. The Political
Resident realized only too well that there were no alternatives
now between force and abject surrender to Theodore, but he
also realized that there would be strong opposition to military
involvement in certain circles at home and therefore decided to
accompany Flad back to England, so as to be able to put the
position clearly to the Government.

He was fortunate in that he had recently been able to appoint
as consul in Massawa a Swiss gentleman, M. Munzinger, who
had lived in Abyssinia for many years and had a detailed knowledge of the country. Munzinger was also an intelligent, educated man of high principles, so that Merewether was able to go
to England in the knowledge that affairs on the spot would be
handled sensibly.

A Conservative Government had taken over from the Whigs
in 1866 and its members like most politicians, were delighted
to declare, more in sorrow than in anger, that the root of the
trouble lay with their inefficient predecessors. This, however,
did not solve the problems of the prisoners. Cameron and his
people had been in close and uncomfortable confinement for

some time, and public opinion was beginning to demand positive action. It was very noticeable that initially at any rate the chief advocates for the use of force were the officers of the Armies in India. The great mutiny of only eight years before had demonstrated to them the value of a sharp military lesson to bring erring native peoples to heel, and they were horrified at the continued forebearance—weakness many chose to call it—of successive home governments. This, they argued, was the way to lose face—and possibly the way to lose an Empire. If one petty ruler could flout a great nation with apparent impunity, others might be tempted to try the same technique.

These views had a profound effect on public opinion in England, but the Government were still disposed to try tact or bribery. It seemed to them that the provision of a few European engineers and some machinery might perhaps mollify Theodore and cause him to release his captives. In November 1866, a civil engineer and six skilled artisans were actually embarked at Southampton with several thousand pounds' worth of machinery. They sailed as far as Massawa where they hung about for six months, by which time it was clear that they could do no good and they were returned to England. Nothing more was heard of this particular part of the plan. In view of the publicity given to the bad treatment of the prisoners already in Theodore's hands, it is remarkable that anyone could have been persuaded to volunteer to go to Abyssinia; the inducement offered must have been considerable. The Government had probably realized after the briefest estimate of the likely cost of a military expedition, that almost any alternative would prove cheaper in the long run.

In April 1867 Lord Stanley, the Foreign Secretary, made one final bid to secure the release of the prisoners by peaceful means. The invaluable Flad was sent off with yet another tactful letter to Theodore, which said that of course the Government would be only too delighted to help a friendly ruler to modernize his country and would certainly supply him with all the men and materials he required. The only stipulation was that first the prisoners must be delivered unharmed to Massawa.

In view of the difficulties of communication it was decided

to allow a full three months to elapse for a reply to be received before any further action was taken, and having thus successfully shelved the need to take a firm decision for at least another quarter, the Government turned its attention to other matters. The Foreign Secretary, however, did take the sensible precaution of inviting the attention of the Secretaries of State for War and India to the possibility that military action might eventually be required.

Colonel Merewether, realizing that in all probability force would have to be employed, set about obtaining all relevant information concerning Abyssinia on which to base plans. There was not in fact a great deal available, although in the manner of the times a considerable number of travellers there had subsequently produced voluminous books, in which they related their experiences and dealt with various aspects of the country in great (if not always accurate) detail. These books he obtained and dissected, and their authors, when available, were also questioned closely on matters likely to affect a military expedition. Other travellers who had not written books were also examined carefully so that presently, by patient sifting and cross-checking, a general but moderately accurate account of conditions in Abyssinia began to appear. One of the big problems was that none of the travellers concerned were professional soldiers and were not therefore able to visualize the problems likely to arise when moving a large army. Merewether himself fortunately had a good basis of practical military experience so that he was able to repair this deficiency to some extent. He found M. Munzinger a particularly useful contact since his long experience of the country, and the fluency with which he spoke Amharic, opened up a number of reliable local sources of information which might never otherwise have been found.

The three broad facts which had first to be established were where to land, where to establish a base, and what route to use into the interior. Although the third could hardly be investigated in detail until a decision had been reached as to whether an expedition would in fact be sent, Merewether was able to accumulate a great deal of useful information regarding the first two. His first estimate of the sort of force required was of the order of some six thousand men, and included one British and six Indian infantry battalions, a brigade of Indian cavalry, a company of sappers, two field batteries, and a troop of Horse Artillery. This, it should be noted, was an unofficial estimate made by a relatively junior officer acting in a political capacity.

As the deadline drew near it also became necessary for the Government to decide how the troops were to be provided should an expedition finally be despatched. The first possibility was to employ home-based units from the United Kingdom, but this offered some disadvantages. Regiments in England were in general smaller than those overseas and were composed largely of young, unseasoned soldiers. Moreover the political climate in Europe was uncertain and ministers were reluctant to advise the removal of such a large body of men for such a remote operation. Transport to the theatre of operations would be difficult (the Suez Canal was not then complete), as would maintenance thereafter. Such a force would also need a secure, well-equipped base in which to organize and acclimatize, and none existed. Aden, it is true, was geographically suitable but its facilities were few; in particular lack of water appeared to preclude its use for such a considerable body.

The second, and much more attractive, possibility was to employ troops from India. Since the Mutiny, India had become the biggest single responsibility for the Army and the pick of its units were stationed there. British battalions were strong in manpower and well acclimatized, and although the mutiny had left a certain natural distrust of the Native Army as a whole, a very great part of it had in fact remained loyal.

If India was to provide the troops, it appeared both from geographical situation and port facilities, that those of the Bombay Presidency would be the most suitable. The native Regiments there were not only reliable and well trained but were also less caste-ridden than many of those in the other Presidencies, and very much more ready to serve overseas. The civil population too was on the whole well-disposed and peaceable, so that a proportion of British units could safely be made available without unduly prejudicing internal security arrangements. Shipping and supplies of all kinds were also available in the sort of quantities likely to be required. It was thus decided to base the expedition—if indeed one was to be sent—on Bombay, and on 10th July 1867 the Secretary of State for India telegraphed the Governor, Mr Seymour Fitzgerald, requesting him to examine the problem in all its aspects and to indicate what size force would be required and how soon it could be made ready. Even at this stage it was made clear that information only was required, and no orders were given for any preparations to be made.

It should be said here that the employment of Indian military forces outside the country posed no serious contitutional problems; the only requirement was that any order for such action despatched to the authorities in India had to be communicated to Parliament within three months.

The Governor, who was primarily a politician had little military knowledge so he turned at once to the man who could best advise him, the Commander-in-Chief of the Bombay Presidency Army, at that time, Lieutenant-General Sir Robert Napier. There was then no suggestion that Napier should command the expedition. He was simply asked for professional guidance as the senior military officer available.

Napier was an officer with an excellent reputation and record. He was the son of a soldier who had died of wounds received in Java in 1811, only a few months after his son was born. He entered Addiscombe, the College for East India Company Military Cadets, in 1824 when he was fourteen, and two years later was commissioned into the Bengal Sappers and Miners. Thereafter his rise had at first been steady rather than spectacular, but he had managed to combine a good deal of active service with much experience of public works, road-building, and the like in remote corners of India, both of which were later to stand him in good stead. His real chance came with the Mutiny, when he was successively Chief-of-Staff to Outram at Lucknow, and then a Brigadier under Sir Hugh Rose in the long pursuit of Tantia Tope. He had also commanded a division in China in the War of 1860, and had assumed his present appointment five years later.

57

All in all, Napier was well qualified to provide the sort of brief required, but before he could do so, he himself needed a good deal of detailed information on conditions in Abyssinia, and his first act was to send for Colonel Phayre, his Quartermaster-General, and instruct him to assemble all the available facts in an easily digested form. It may be queried, why his Quartermaster-General? The answer is that the staff system in the British Army was then in something of a state of flux; there was no General Staff in the modern sense, but in India, commanders generally worked on the Wellingtonian system of making the Quartermaster-General's branch responsible for intelligence and operations.

Phayre, like his Commander-in-Chief, was ideally suited to the task, for apart from his very considerable military abilities he was also something of a geographer and explorer. He was moreover a man of boundless energy whose iron constitution had not apparently been affected in the least by a jagged Baluchi musketball through the lungs at Meanee nearly a quarter of a century before. He was an experienced and enthusiastic hill walker and had the reputation of being able to cross the most difficult country on foot at a speed which quickly reduced active young officers half his age to a state of exhaustion.

Phayre very soon assembled and digested all the information available in Bombay and produced a brief but extremely lucid report for General Napier. It is not clear whether he had conferred with Merewether at this stage, although as they were well known to each other it is highly probable that he had done so. Whichever the case, they both came to the same theoretical conclusions; namely that the best course would probably be a landing in the vicinity of Massawa followed by a southward thrust along one of the several passes known to lead up on to the main plateau.

Some indication of the lack of co-ordination of staff duties at the time is given by the fact that a third officer, Colonel Cooke of the Topographical Department of the War Office, was also busy assembling information; again it is not known whether he and the other two officers pooled their knowledge but in this case it seems unlikely.

Napier did not waste any time, and by 23rd July he had produced a memorandum which dealt with every aspect of the proposed expedition in considerable detail. He realized only too well that much of the information on which his proposals were based was conjectural, and thus his first recommendation was that a reconnaissance party should be despatched to the country as soon as the decision to send an expedition was finally made, in order to clear up the many gaps in his geographical knowledge.

On political grounds he was a good deal more certain of his facts. He wrote:

It appears that by his misconduct Theodorus has made enemies of all his neighbours, and that the people of Tigri on the North, and the Gallas on the South and West, would readily join against him; that his resources and followers are much reduced and it is believed by some that a small compact force, well-equipped with carriage, could safely make its way to Magdala, overthrow Theodorus, and release the prisoners.

All this is probably the case but may not remain so. The Emperor, seeing his danger, may reconcile himself with his enemies, intriguers of other nations may raise hostility against us. We should neither like to be the means of the pagan Gallas overwhelming the miserable representation of Christianity in Africa, nor of making use of some portion of the people, who might suffer, after our departure, the terrible vengeance which is dealt out to their enemies, when in their power, by the barbarous races of Abyssinia.

An expedition, though making such friends and obtaining such assistance as would prevent molestation, must be sufficiently strong to do its own work with ease and security.

His estimate of the force required was a good deal larger than that made by Merewether. It would be necessary to establish a firm base and hold a series of defended posts along the line of communication, while still leaving sufficient troops available to deal with Magdala; this he reckoned would require twelve thousand fighting men, exclusive of followers.

Little was known about the actual resources of the country.

59

Given the goodwill and co-operation of the local inhabitants along the line of operations it might be possible to obtain meat, grain, forage, and fuel in some quantities, but there was no way of making even a rough estimate of how large these quantities would be. The force would have to be planned on a virtually self-sufficient basis—at least to start with—and this would require transport in enormous quantities. In view of the uncertainty regarding the state of paths in the interior, carriage would have to consist in the main of pack mules and horses, although camels and even bullocks might be used. It was considered that some local transport might be available on a contract basis.

Lastly Napier considered that it might take about three months to assemble and organize the sort of force he envisaged. Transport would of course take longer to procure in the quantities required, and as it was clear that the whole success of any expedition was going to depend on the effective transporting of supplies, he recommended that agents with ample funds should be spread over Southern Europe and the Middle East as quickly as possible in order to start purchasing animals and assembling them in suitable depots.

The size and complexity of the problem must have dismayed the British Government, since the expedition was clearly going to be an extremely expensive one. The Government of India Act of 1858 prescribed, moreover, that except for preventing or repelling actual invasion the revenues of India were not to be used to defray the costs of any external expedition, so that it was clear that all expenses would have to be met by the British taxpayer. Nevertheless the Government went on with it, as indeed they were morally bound to do. On 25th July orders were sent to Bombay to organize and despatch a reconnaissance force of the type proposed by Napier, while at the same time the Foreign Office made the necessary arrangements to enable them to land on what was technically Egyptian territory. A few days later instructions were also telegraphed to begin the purchase of transport animals.

The final decision to despatch a force was announced on 13th August 1867. Disraeli, then Chancellor of the Exchequer, announced in his flowery way that the expedition would probably cost about two million pounds to assemble on African soil, and perhaps a further million and a half if the King's continued intransigence made it necessary to proceed as far as Magdala. There were, he agreed, certain imponderables which might add something to the cost, particularly if the expedition had not been completed by the end of April, but he assured his listeners that the estimates, although rough, were not careless and were submitted with "a confidence by no means slight".

The next requirement was to decide who was to command the expedition, and although the final decision rested with the Government it was the duty of the Commander-in-Chief to submit suitable names for consideration. The Duke of Cambridge was a conscientious man and gave the problem careful consideration. It was the sort of post eagerly sought after by ambitious soldiers, since success would probably mean a peerage and other benefits; in the fashion of the day there was some lobbying.

In this particular case it was vital that the man chosen should be amongst the best available, since this would inevitably be a shop-window affair demonstrating the new administrative efficiency of the British Army, and failure was unthinkable. Merewether was considered briefly, for he had a good reputation and had been concerned with the affair from the start, but he was far too junior for the size of force proposed. He was however given the important task of commanding the reconnaissance force. Other names and records were examined and rejected, until finally the Duke of Cambridge came to the sensible conclusion that Napier himself was the proper man for the command. Napier had done the preliminary planning; he was a scientific soldier with a flair for administration, and at the same time had a good record as a fighting commander. That he was inclined to be cautious and methodical rather than dashing was an added point in his favour—dashing officers were always liable to get into serious scrapes and the last thing either the Government or the Horse Guards could afford was a disaster.

All this had of course been considered earlier, so Napier was nominated on 14th August. His instructions from the Government were extraordinarily slight. He was to "Make a peremptory demand for the delivery of the captives, and to follow it up by such measures as he thinks expedient."

*   *   *

Once the final decision had been taken the Government made every effort to ensure the eventual success of the expedition. Napier was given *carte blanche* to a degree previously unheard of, and all the resources of a modern industrial state were at once brought into play.

Hundreds of ships were chartered, many at high rates. Some were equipped with condensers so as to provide a secure water supply on the dry, inhospitable, Red Sea littoral; others were fitted out as hospital ships to deal with casualties and sick. It was generally believed that these, particularly the sick, would be numerous, for Africa was associated in the minds of most people with a variety of dread diseases and it was generally supposed that Abyssinia would be hideously unhealthy. The insurance world certainly believed so, and officers detailed for the expedition found that their premiums rocketed at the mere mention of their destination.

The necessary equipment for a railway was assembled at Bombay, as were miles and miles of iron waterpipe; condensers and water pumps of the most modern pattern were ordered from the United States, while simultaneously a steady flow of the more usual kinds of military stores was directed towards the Red Sea.

In the meantime numerous purchasing officers were scouring the Mediterranean and Middle Eastern countries for transport animals—mainly mules—and muleteers. They were amply supplied with funds, which was just as well, for the sudden demand sent prices rocketing. A number of horse transports were kept cruising round the main Mediterranean ports, and a large animal depot was established at Alexandria by a detachment of the Military Train; from here the animals were sent by rail to Suez for onward shipment to the Red Sea coast.

The selection of the actual units for the force presented comparatively little difficulty, since Napier, as Commander-in-Chief, already had a close knowledge of the troops available. The balance between British and Indian troops, however, had to be adjusted with some care. The Mutiny was less than ten years old, and although only the Bengal Army had been affected, there was a natural disposition to distrust the Native Army as a whole. The general policy was that one-third of the troops in India should be British, a proportion which included all the artillery with the exception of a few mountain guns; it was not therefore desirable to withdraw too large a number of British troops for the expedition. Nor would it have been sensible on other grounds. Napier, although himself originally a Company man, had seen too much of British troops in the Mutiny to have any hesitations as to their worth—on purely fighting qualities they were probably at least twice (and possibly three times) as good as the bulk of the native regiments. He also realized, however, that the Abyssinians were unlikely to prove sufficiently skilled fighters as to make this an important consideration. The Bombay native troops had a good reputation, and being accustomed to a hot climate were much less likely to suffer from disease or heat exhaustion than even seasoned British soldiers. They were also accustomed to looking after themselves and living much more frugally than the British, so that their requirements for transport and camp followers would be much less than those necessary for European troops—an important consideration in Abyssinia.

The final composition of the force therefore was: half a British cavalry regiment and four of Indian cavalry; one battery of nine-pounder guns, three of mountain guns (one of the latter being native), and two heavy mortars; one company of British engineers and seven of native sappers and miners; and four British and ten Indian infantry battalions. Although at first it had been intended to raise the whole force from the Bombay Presidency, it eventually became necessary to include a proportion from both Bengal and Madras. The final list of units is shown in Appendix A.

An important accession to the firepower of the infantry was the decision to rearm the British element with breech-loading rifles. The value of such weapons had been amply demonstrated in both the American Civil War and the more recent Austro-Prussian War of 1866. All European armies were busy experimenting with them.

Until 1867 the standard British infantry weapon had been the Enfield, an excellent rifle of its type, very accurate to about four hundred yards and capable of effective collective fire at well over twice that distance. It was, however, a muzzle-loader and consequently slow to operate. It was charged by means of a paper cartridge containing powder and bullet, but required a separate percussion cap. In order to load an Enfield, it was necessary to place the hammer at half cock, tear the end off the cartridge and pour the powder down the muzzle, put the bullet in the muzzle, tear away the surplus paper, and ram down. A cap was then placed on the nipple, the hammer drawn back to full cock, and the piece fired. When allowances were made for careful aim, and for the problems of ramming down the bullet when the barrel was hot and foul from previous discharges, a fair rate of fire was probably two or three rounds a minute.

Experiments with various breech-loaders had begun early in the British service, but in order not to drop behind in the race, conversion of the Enfield rifle to breech-loading had begun in 1867 as a temporary expedient. This was done by cutting away two or three inches from the breech end of the barrel and attaching a form of breech mechanism invented by a Dutchman called Snider. The new breech consisted of a semi-circular trough, closed by a solid steel block hinged on the right. The new rifle fired a cartridge with a brass case and integral percussion cap on modern lines; the striker, which passed diagonally through the block, was operated by the original Enfield hammer, and the block was so designed that it also formed an extractor to withdraw the empty case from the breech into the chamber, whence it was thrown clear by turning the rifle over to the right.

Like most makeshifts, the Snider was not wholly satisfactory. Nevertheless it was a reasonably efficient mechanism which doubled—or in good hands trebled—the rate of fire of its parent muzzle-loader with no corresponding disadvantages. This was particularly important for the Abyssinian expedition, because the native troops, as a matter of policy, had been armed with obsolete and comparatively ineffective smoothbores since the Mutiny.

Four thousand infantry pattern Sniders were soon on their way to India, together with a thousand carbines for the cavalry and artillery. In view of their probable role, permission was given also to arm a proportion of the native cavalry with these weapons. Two and a half million rounds of ammunition, packed in seventy pound boxes suitable for mule carriage, were also despatched. In order to increase his firepower still further Napier requested permission to rearm a proportion of his native infantry with the discarded Enfields of the British regiments. There was, however, great reluctance to place rifled weapons in the hands of the Indian troops, and although permission was eventually grudgingly given it did not reach Napier until the expedition was almost over.

The artillery for the force consisted of one battery of Armstrong breech-loading nine-pounders, drawn in the normal way by teams of eight horses, and three mountain batteries. The British artillery was then in process of being reorganized, and although the one native battery was a permanently organized unit, the two British units were formed in the old-fashioned way by taking garrison companies from India and giving them guns from England and locally purchased mules. The expedition occurred during the remarkable period in which the British army, having experimented with breech-loading guns, had decided to revert to muzzle-loaders. The new steel mountain guns were of this pattern, and were thus in theory more modern than the breech-loading Armstrongs.

In view of the possibility of siege type operations against Magdala, Napier also included two eight inch mortars in his artillery.

An Indian army also required a great number of followers— cooks, servants, watercarriers, sanitary men, grass-cutters, and a host of others, who usually far outnumbered the actual combatant element, and this was initially the case with the expedition to Abyssinia although they were to be pruned drastically later.

The real problem, however, came over the organization of the

E

vast transport corps on which the success of the whole expedition would ultimately depend. General Napier, a most practical soldier, had strong views on the matter. In the first place he considered it essential that the corps should be a military one; the individual muleteers themselves might not be soldiers (although they would have to be subject to some form of military discipline) but there must be a sound military framework. There was more involved than the simple transport of loads from A to B. The mules had to be fed and cared for, and it must be possible to detach small numbers of muleteers for isolated duties without loss of efficiency, waste of time, or pillaging of loads.

The Bombay Government quibbled over the transport corps both as regards strength and organization. The Commissariat department obviously feared that the new Corps—which was technically within their province—was to be an independent organization, almost a rival, under the direct control of the Quartermaster-General. They made their views widely known and seem to have had the ear of both the Governor and the Council, so that Napier, sensing that he was likely to be overruled, did not press his own ideas, but merely reserved the right to comment on the proposed organization when it was ready.

When he saw the suggestions for the Corps his worst fears were realized. It was clearly badly organized and far too small for the tasks envisaged, and in particular no provision had been made for controlling the individuals comprising it. Napier expressed himself forcibly on 9th September 1867:

> I believe the success of systems depends more on the men who work them than on the systems themselves. . . . But I cannot accept without protest a decision to throw such a body of men as the drivers of our transport animals will be—if we get them—on an expedition in a foreign country without a very complete organization to ensure discipline and good order.

The real problem was that those responsible could not divorce themselves from the sort of expedition with which they were familiar—a leisurely perambulation across the fertile plains of India; Napier continued—

The Commissariat department have but a small quantity of their own carriage to manage; the greater portion has been hired carriage, managed under a sort of social organization peculiar to itself, which has existed from time immemorial, and which goes on somehow, one hardly knows how. . . .

His vigorous and well-reasoned criticisms made some impression on the Governor, but by then much time had been wasted and it was too late to do much about it. In the event, the Corps had to be largely reorganized on the lines originally envisaged by Napier during the course of the actual operations.

By this time mules, horses, ponies, bullocks, and camels were beginning to assemble at the depots in large numbers. Over eight thousand animals were purchased in a few weeks and the various ships detailed to carry them were kept busy. The bullocks came mostly from Bombay and the camels, unlike the other animals, were not purchased but hired from contractors in neighbouring Arab countries. A number of Government elephants were also despatched from Bombay to carry the mortars and Armstrong guns, should it not be possible to get them forward by normal draught.

Transport officers and non-commissioned officers, mostly volunteers from regiments serving in India, packed their kits and started on their way. Shiploads of packsaddles began to arrive, as did veterinary surgeons drawn from military garrisons all over the Empire. Muleteers, and individuals claiming to be muleteers, were also taken on in considerable numbers. The raw material was beginning to appear, but it was going to require organization of the highest order to convert this strange mixture of men, material, and animals into an effective Corps. Fortunately the Government of Bengal, which from its geographical situation had some experience of mountain warfare, offered two properly organized and well disciplined mountain trains, one from Lahore and one from Rawalpindi. These were high calibre units, in which the men were keen, capable, and thoroughly reliable and the mules healthy and well cared for. They were among the few units ready to take the field immediately, and it is a remarkable thing that in the last stages of preparation for a campaign which would rely for its success almost entirely on an efficient transport organization, this relative handful of men and mules constituted the only part of the corps capable of carrying out its functions.

CHAPTER 5
Preliminary Arrangements

T HE reconnaissance of the coastal strip and passes up onto the plateau was entrusted to a committee under the presidency of Colonel Merewether: its permanent members were Colonel Phayre the QMG, and Colonel Wilkins of the Royal Engineers, the senior Naval Officer and senior Medical Officer being co-opted as required. Apart from these, the party included a number of other more junior officers—including A and Q staff officers, a Commissariat representative, and two Engineers, together with an assortment of minor tradesmen, sappers, works overseers, clerks, and others. The military force consisted of a company of the Bombay Marine battalion and an escort of forty Sabres of the 3rd Bombay Cavalry under a *subahdar*. There were also the usual numbers of public and private followers, grooms, grass-cutters, servants, muleteers, tent *lascars* and the like, and a hundred and forty-nine mules allowed for baggage.

Before the reconnaissance party sailed on 17th September 1867, Merewether was given a memorandum for his guidance by General Napier. Wilkins, the sapper representative of the committee (who later wrote a book describing his experiences with the party) referred to this memorandum as a remarkable document and anyone reading it today must be struck by both its breadth and its detail. Although based on scanty and not always accurate information it predicted the whole course of the expedition with remarkable accuracy, and dealt with all the major contingencies likely to occur. It is printed in full in Appendix B, so all that it is necessary to say here is that it covered the questions of a harbour, shore installations, the location of the base depot, camps generally, animal transport, food and forage, the possible need for higher altitude camps for the British element if delays occurred, the need for a cart-road on to the plateau, and a host of other relevant matters.

Various experts had already offered their suggestions regarding landing-places and lines of approach, and these had to be considered carefully. Sir Samuel Baker, the Egyptian explorer, had suggested a route in via Metemma, but this was long, communications were difficult, and it might lead to political complications if the Abyssinians felt that they were being invaded from the territory of their traditional enemy. Dr Krapf suggested an approach from Tadjura in what later became French Somaliland, but although this was a shorter route it involved crossing a wide expanse of waterless desert. General Coughlan, sometime Commander-in-Chief in Aden, and an officer who had had modest hopes of being selected to command the force, proposed Massawa, while Dr Beke suggested Annesley Bay, about thirty miles further south.

The first and obvious place to be investigated seemed to be Massawa, but on close examination it soon became apparent that the lack of water would prove an insurmountable problem, so the party continued down to Annesley Bay, and landed at the small village of Mulkutto near Zula, on the site of the ancient Greek Adulis. The bay, open to the north only, provided a good and sheltered anchorage, although the shore sloped so gently that two hundred yards out there was often less than four feet of water. After some difficulty with the animals they succeeded in landing and soon found fresh water in fair quantities. The area was not attractive, since it consisted of a wide, desolate, sandy plain, dotted with rocks and coarse shrubs and seamed with dry water-courses. Behind it rose the mountains, ridge upon ridge, up into the clouds; beyond the mountains—almost four hundred miles beyond—was their objective, Magdala. The real advantage of the place was that the salty waterless plain was only fourteen miles wide, and thus did not offer a serious barrier to movement.

Reconnaissance started at once, but on the assumption that Zula would in fact be the point of disembarkation it was clear that the first requirement was for a jetty. There was no suitable stone available on the Western side of the bay, but local native boats and boatmen were hired in large numbers and an adequate supply soon began to accumulate from further afield. The sappers first marked out the proposed line of the jetty by pegging fascines to the sea bed; stone walls were then built outside these and the space between them filled with loose stone. Three hundred yards were constructed in a remarkably short time, and at that distance from shore there was always a guaranteed five feet of water, ships' boats and lighters were soon able to tie up alongside. Later an artificial island of considerable size was built at the end of the jetty to accommodate a large condenser plant, and a tramway was laid along it to the beach. Later still a second jetty was also constructed.

By 11th October the energetic Quartermaster-General had been to Kumayli at the foot of one of the known passes, and had then pushed up it to a place called Suru where he found water. He reported that the track, although difficult, could be made passable. Colonel Wilkins went up to inspect it and was appalled; he described the narrow pass as being blocked by "a boulder the size of a villa, resting against others nearly as large".

Phayre, however, knew it was passable. While examining the obstruction he had watched with interest as a herd of cattle was driven down it, and later actually saw a party of the local tribesmen drive a troop of laden bullocks up it. Some of the worst places had been improved by primitive ramps of rock and rough timber, and he considered that they could easily be improved still more. He recommended to Merewether that work should start at once, but the latter decided to wait until he had completed a reconnaissance of some of the likely alternatives further south, which if suitable would reduce the overall length of the journey. Merewether, therefore, set out on 21st October and spent a fruitless and uncomfortable fourteen days in a hot, waterless plain, glittering with salt crystals and littered with jagged rocks. At the end of it he gave up, and settled for villa-sized boulders at Suru as an acceptable alternative.

71

A few days later the Royal Navy arrived in the shape of HMS *Satellite* commanded by Captain Edye. Edye at once put himself and his ship at the disposal of the Army, and as a supply of water was the first essential, he made arrangements for condensing it in considerable quantities and pumping it ashore.

The advance brigade landed from Bombay at the end of October. It consisted of the 3rd Light Cavalry, the 10th Native Infantry, a mountain battery, two companies of sappers, and elements of the Commissariat Corps. It was commanded by Colonel Field of the 10th Native Infantry who had been appointed local Brigadier-General for the purpose, but although this made him the senior officer present he had firm orders not to interfere with the reconnaissance force but to do all he could to assist it. This might have proved difficult, but the officers knew and respected each other and this saved the day; Field placed himself virtually under Merewether's orders and all was well.

The cavalry were quickly moved to a camp some twenty miles further west where good water existed, while most of the remainder of the advance brigade were at once set to work road making, leaving only a few details to set up the base.

As soon as the route was passable, Merewether moved the bulk of the brigade up to Senafé, the point at which the track finally emerged on to the Abyssinian plateau. It was some sixty miles inland and seven thousand feet above sea level, and although re-supply was difficult he considered it tactically essential that the place should be held. Even more essential was the need to establish friendly relations with the Abyssinians and encourage them to bring their local produce in for sale to the Commissariat. This it was hoped would be achieved by a combination of strict discipline and financial generosity.

The horses of the 3rd Cavalry were then struck with an epidemic of African glanders, a swift and deadly disease which killed them in large numbers. It gave no warning. Loss of appetite was followed by swelling of the head and neck and then death, often in great agony, in a matter of hours. The regiment was also pushed on up to Senafé in the hope that the higher altitude and better climate would save the remaining animals. This in fact was the result, but as the regiment lost some seventy per cent of its horses before the epidemic was over, it was for a time quite ineffective as a mounted unit. A purchasing officer was sent to Egypt to buy remounts, and as animals of fair quality were reasonably plentiful it was not long before the regiment was again fit for action. Fortunately the disease—for which there was no cure—did not affect camels or cattle, though it killed mules as swiftly as it did horses.

* * *

Back at Zula the situation was rapidly becoming chaotic. Brigadier-General Field had gone forward with the bulk of his brigade and the members of the committee were still involved in route reconnaissance. There was thus no firm central control in the base, no adequate labour force, nor—in some quarters— any real sense of urgency. H. M. Stanley (who later achieved considerable fame as an African explorer and whose greeting to Dr Livingstone still constitutes one of the best known clichés of the English language), went to Abyssinia as War Correspondent for the *New York Herald*. He was very much a man of the people himself; British by birth, raised in a workhouse, and thus unlikely to be biased in favour of the officer class as a whole. Nevertheless his later reporting was in general so fair that it is difficult to accuse him of any early bias, and it seems likely that his picture of a portion of the Commissariat in action is a fair one. Bewhiskered officers lounged in pyjamas in their lux-urious tents, fanning themselves languidly; visitors were quizzed through glasses and, if apparently acceptable, were offered boundless liquid hospitality in true Indian style before being ushered out with a cool "Ta-ta ole fellah," without having achieved much. The picture is cruel, but the species recognizable. Stanley himself was quick to add that these "brittle gentry" bore no relation to the "many officers devoted to their duties" whom he found further forward. It may be one of the inevitable features of war that this should be so; certainly it is a pheno-menon which has struck many other people since Stanley's day.

Stores and equipment of all kinds were beginning to accumulate on the beach in indescribable but, unhappily, rather familiar confusion; any experienced French soldier who landed at that moment would have taken one long look, murmured "Encore la Crimée," and departed with the scornful conviction that another shambles was imminent. At the time a good many British officers might have agreed.

The greatest immediate cause for concern was the state of the animals. Transports were pouring into Annesley Bay and discharging vast numbers of mules, horses, and camels, for which there was neither forage nor adequate water. A few so-called muleteers were available, but the bulk of them (some three hundred) were the off-scourings of the slums of Bombay; they had absolutely no knowledge of animal management and no desire to learn. Most of the remainder of the muleteers had volunteered for service with the mules they had sold and amongst them were Indians, Spaniards, Persians, Egyptians, Turks, Afghans, Arabs, Albanians, Frenchmen, Italians, and even one or two Germans. The majority were Persian and Egyptian, confirmed trouble makers who struck at the slightest provocation and were of little use. Even the few willing and competent ones amongst the other nationalities, having neither proper central control nor any common language, could achieve little.

Animals were bundled ashore with nothing except rope halters, so that even the few that were initially properly secured soon gnawed their way free, and presently the whole area was swarming with loose mules, horses, and camels, many diseased and all suffering from thirst and hunger. The navy rigged up troughs ashore, and when these were filled with water pumped into them from the condensers the maddened animals galloped up and fought each other savagely in their anxiety to drink. Many never got a fair share and soon began to weaken, a process accelerated by lack of forage. The first to die were the big Spanish mules; they were mostly stall-fed beasts which had been used for drawing carts in the larger towns, and they had no notion of foraging for themselves. The purchasing officers had been told that thirteen hands was the lower limit for mules, and as many of them had little knowledge of the beasts, they had tended to work on the assumption of "the bigger, the better," although in practice it did not prove a sound philosophy. Many of the other mules were tougher and more self-reliant, and so lasted longer, but soon they too began to die and presently the desert for miles round the base was littered with swollen carcases. By day they attracted hundreds of vultures; by night the hyenas and jackals came out to feast on the unexpected bounty, not always waiting until their victims were dead. Corruption followed as a matter of course and in a few days the whole area was buzzing with flies and foul with the smell of rotting flesh.

Fortunately for all concerned, the next convoy brought in the Sind Brigade. It consisted of the 33rd Duke of Wellington's Regiment, the Baluchi Regiment, and the battery of Armstrong guns. It was commanded by Brigadier-General Collings who had just been promoted from command of the 33rd. Even more fortunate was the fact that with this convoy also came Major-General Sir Charles Staveley; he had been nominated to command the 1st Division when formed, and had been sent ahead by Napier to make various preliminary arrangements. Napier made no mistake when his choice fell on Staveley. Staveley was then fifty, an infantryman who had fought in the Crimea and in China (when he had nominated "Chinese" Gordon to command the Chinese Army), and an energetic and capable administrator into the bargain. He came ashore and looked in horror at the chaos around him; then he mounted a horse and made a quick but careful survey of the camp to decide what to do first. Things began to move in Zula from that moment.

The 33rd Regiment scrambled onto the pier from the lighters and marched off to the beach, strangely dressed in sun-helmets, khaki drill trousers, and scarlet frocks; they were the first European troops to set foot on that particular shore since de Gama's ill-fated musketeers three and a quarter centuries before.

Staveley seized on them gladly and set them to work rounding up mules, and the battalion threw off its hot red coats, rolled up its sleeves, and set to work with customary vigour. The heat on the plain was intense but they were accustomed to it, for they had been under command of an officer with advanced views on tropical hygiene. At a time when most British troops in India spent the noonday hours in their barrack-rooms in heat and boredom, the 33rd had been encouraged to get out and take exercise, and now the wisdom of the policy became obvious. After a couple of days of hard work and hard swearing (the regiment was almost equally famed for both) the surviving animals were tethered in neat lines, this time with chains, and were being systematically watered and fed. Forage was still scarce, but enough was being brought ashore to keep the remaining beasts in fair condition.

The 33rd then had a few days respite to settle in and make its various preparations for the campaign. One of the most important of these was in the matter of arms. The other European troops had drawn their Sniders in India but there had been no time for the 33rd to do so and it had thus landed still armed with muzzle-loaders. These were soon withdrawn and replaced by breech-loaders and the troops at once set to work to master their new weapons. Fortunately the Snider breech was a simple mechanism and it did not take long for experienced soldiers to understand it. As far as sight-setting, aiming, and firing was concerned the new rifle was identical with its parent Enfield.

Another odd problem must have been the assimilation of a draft of ninety Germans. They were the remnants of the British foreign legion, raised (but never used) for service in the Crimea. After many adventures in the Cape and elsewhere they had found themselves in the 109th Regiment, whence they were posted to the 33rd for the campaign. A young officer of the Regiment noted that "It was odd to hear their non-commissioned officers talking German in the orderly room and having to use an interpreter," and it is obvious that the integration of such stubborn aliens, good soldiers though they may have been, must have given rise to all sorts of difficulties.

*   *   *

The local tribesmen were a nomadic people, the Shohos; they hovered between the Egyptian plain and the Abyssinian uplands with little regard for man-made boundaries, although they owed a technical allegiance to the Egyptians. Like most nomadic people they were extremely primitive and poor, and in order to augment their incomes they habitually resorted to banditry. They were by no means a brave people but they could swoop down in numbers and rob small parties, trusting to their speed and agility in the hills to get them clear of trouble if the opposition should prove too strong. In spite of the mutual hatred of Abyssinians and Egyptians there had always been some trade between them, but of recent years the depredations of the Shohos had become so serious that the north-eastern trade routes had largely fallen into disuse.

At first the nomads were perplexed as to how they might gain advantage from this sudden influx of strangers who from their dress and property were obviously rich, and who apparently had the magical ability to drink seawater and thrive on it. The Shohos had little to offer for sale, and banditry was clearly out of the question against large numbers of well-armed men. General Staveley provided the answer. He required unskilled labour in considerable quantities, and although work was not a concept with which the Shohos were familiar, the temptation held out by the amount of money offered was too strong to resist and they were soon hard at it, digging, carrying, and scavenging. The original idea was to employ them mainly to dispose of the hundreds of putrid carcases in the area, but this the Shohos would not do for any consideration. Eventually small parties of Indian sweepers with teams of mules had to be employed instead and these, working with a will, had the area clear in a very short time.

Colonel Merewether, from his previous experience of the Shohos, also made good use of them. Acting on the well-established principle that poachers make the best gamekeepers he approached the local chiefs and offered them a small monthly subsidy for "protecting" convoys up the pass, a polite euphemism for a bribe to refrain from looting them themselves.

He also employed them as transport. The lack of mules and muleteers had made it difficult to keep the advanced brigade at Senafé supplied, and although a certain amount of food and forage was beginning to reach the Commissariat there, it had so far been impossible to start building up the sort of reserves which General Napier considered essential before any further advance became possible. The Shohos were charmed by the idea. It was more profitable than highway robbery and far less dangerous. They loaded up not only their animals but also their wives and families and sent them plodding off up the pass in exchange for the coveted silver dollars.

The currency of Abyssinia consisted of a single coin, the Austrian Maria Theresa dollar, which had been in circulation for a hundred years and which was still being minted in Vienna. Because of the limited nature of the local trade, and the tendency to hoard dollars under the floors of huts, they were in relatively short supply. There was nothing else; no paper, no banks, no urbane money-lenders to produce coin in exchange for more sophisticated forms of currency. Even gold, although acceptable, quickly went out of circulation, and it thus became a matter of extreme urgency to keep an adequate supply of these coins moving towards the base. Fortunately, they were in general use over much of the Middle East, and British agents were soon busy scouring the area for them.

The Abyssinians were at first very suspicious, even of the familiar dollars. Long experience had made them connoisseurs of the coin and they tended to examine each one carefully to ensure that every detail of the Empress's crown and decoration was complete, that mint marks were clear, and the piece itself not unduly worn. Initially it was not unusual for a native, having accepted a dollar, to bring it back next day and ask for a better one, although as the expedition progressed and more and more cash entered the country they took a more sophisticated attitude and accepted them by the handful with no more than a cursory glance.

Enormous quantities of the dollars were required, and it was not until the Austrian mint obligingly accelerated its rate of production that the problem was solved. Even so there remained the difficulty of carriage and distribution. Maria Theresa dollars were heavy; they averaged about eighteen to the pound, and as hundreds of thousands were required the problems of transport and escort became—and to some extent remained—acute.

The Maria Theresa dollar was technically worth about four shillings, but a currency based on a single coin does not make for flexibility and it was difficult to decide on suitable rates for stores and services. An Abyssinian might demand a dollar for a glass of milk, or equally might ask the same for the whole bucket; shrewd bargaining became the order of the day. In the long run the sudden vast influx of coin into Abyssinia must have reduced their value considerably but this was not important. All that any sensible Abyssinian wanted was to get his hands onto a good share of the miraculous stream while it lasted.

*   *   *

Order and organization quickly appeared in the Zula base. The jetty was finished and furnished with a tramway, and a second pier was started exclusively for Commissariat use. Condensers of the newest type were brought from America and set up on an artificial island, and soon a hundred and twenty tons of water were being pumped ashore daily. The tiny quantities of fresh water normally available ashore were of course quite inadequate for more than a small fraction of the force so that the base was entirely dependant on the condensers. A mechanical failure could therefore have had serious effects, and work was quickly started on erecting a huge prefabricated tank in order to build up a reserve. The normal daily ration was twelve pints per head—no more than the minimum necessary for healthy survival. No fresh water could be spared for bathing, and it was difficult to keep clean, so the jetty became a popular resort for all ranks off duty. One of General Napier's ADCs wrote:

> I used, with many others, to go and bathe off the pier-head . . . as there one always got sufficient amount of water for a header, even at low tide, and anywhere else involved nearly a quarter of a mile out in mud and water. The pier-head was certainly the most public place anywhere, but one soon got used to that. You saw the greatest swells there, the pink of the ballroom, elbowing their way in and

out in man's most natural costume, among all sorts of people in the same condition. . . .

Cropped heads also became the fashion, and the rules regarding shaving were relaxed so that fearsome beards began to sprout on all sides.

Prefabricated huts were landed and erected as stores, and a steady influx of Commissariat personnel did much to ease the considerable store handling problems. The quantities landed were huge, as ship after ship came steaming along the channels carefully buoyed by the Royal Navy, and discharged their cargoes into lighters.

More troops came ashore. The 4th (Kings Own) arrived, as did two more Regiments of Bombay Native Infantry, a battalion of Punjab Pioneers, two companies of sappers, and the mountain gunners. These latter at once found themselves short of reliable drivers for their mules and had to borrow sixty-five men from the 4th (which had been made up with drafts from the 49th and 95th before leaving India and was thus able to spare them).

The newcomers were absorbed quickly. Tents, rations, and water were available and they quickly settled down and were put to work. The base system was not only working, but working so well that it soon had some reserve capacity, and by the end of the year a ration reserve of three months for two thousand Europeans and six months for seven thousand Indians was held, while supplies were also at last beginning to build up at Senafé. Christmas came and went almost unnoticed in the general atmosphere of work, although the officers of at least one company of the 33rd had an excellent meal cooked by the servant of the company commander. Amongst other good things this genius conjured up an excellent plum pudding, made principally from pounded ship's biscuits.

The bulk of the troops were employed on road-building. Much of the work called for no more than heavy unskilled labour—clearing boulders, filling in holes, and marking the line of the track at places where confusion might occur. The bad places were entrusted to the Indian sappers and miners, who achieved near miracles. The worst place was the wild jumble of huge boulders in the narrow pass at Suru, known locally as the Devil's Staircase, but it was ready for wheeled traffic in six weeks, a remarkable feat achieved entirely by steady pick and shovel work without mechanical aids.

Colonel Wilkins' graphic description of boulders "the size of a villa" was no exaggeration and obstacles of such magnitude could neither be moved nor blown up. The course adopted was to select a suitable line for the path, then build containing walls of loose stone across the gaps between boulders and fill in the space between with rock and rubble. The method was not new; it had been used regularly in India, and Napier himself had suggested that it might be the answer without even seeing the obstacle.

The final result was an elevated but well-graded road, ten feet wide and perfectly practicable for artillery and even bullock carts. It was however strictly a dry weather route, for in the rainy season the narrow pass became a roaring torrent at times, rolling huge rocks before it like marbles, so that six weeks work might well be swept away in as many hours. If this happened it would also isolate the advanced brigade—the reason why everyone was so anxious to establish adequate dumps on the plateau. The rains were not due for some months, but there was always the faint risk of a freak downpour before the usual time.

*　　*　　*

On the political side things were also going well. Early in October, Sir Robert Napier had judged the time right to despatch a proclamation to Theodore, reiterating the demand for the release of the prisoners and stating categorically that should this not be done he proposed to enter Abyssinia with an army to free them. It was made clear that there was no desire to affect his sovereignty, but the sting was in the tail:

Should they not be delivered safely into my hands, should they suffer a continuance of ill-treatment, or should any injury befall them, your Majesty will be held personally

F　　　　　　　　　　　　　　　　　　　　81

responsible, and no hope of future condonation need be entertained.

A second proclamation was issued simultaneously to the Governors, Chiefs, Religious orders, and people of Abyssinia:

It is known to you that Theodorus, King of Abyssinia, detains in captivity the British consul Cameron, the British envoy Rassam, and many others, in violation of the laws of all civilized nations.

All friendly persuasion having failed to obtain their release, my Sovereign has commanded me to lead an Army to liberate them.

All who have befriended the prisoners or assist them in their liberation shall be well rewarded, but those who may injure them shall be severely punished.

When the time shall arise for the march of a British Army through your country, bear in mind, People of Abyssinia, that the Queen of England has no unfriendly feelings towards you and no design against your country or your liberty.

Your religious establishments, your persons, and property shall be carefully protected.

All supplies required for my soldiers shall be paid for. No peaceable inhabitants shall be molested. The sole object for which the British Force has been sent to Abyssinia is the liberation of Her Majesty's subjects.

There is no intention to occupy permanently any portion of Abyssinian Territory, or to interfere with the Government of the country.

Several copies of the letter to Theodore were despatched to him by various messengers although it is not clear whether he ever received any of them. One reached Rassam who, perhaps prudently, promptly destroyed it lest it should further anger the King. The second, general proclamation, however had an immediate effect, and it was then that the wisdom of the early occupation of Senafé became apparent.

Word of the moderation, generosity, and fair dealing of the strangers had spread rapidly across the plateau as news does in a primitive country, and this practical demonstration of the good faith of the proclamation went far to convince the Abyssinians of Napier's sincerity.

Their real fear was of permanent occupation. They were at heart isolationists, and although they would tolerate, indeed even welcome, the British in the short term, they would be even more delighted to see their backs as soon as their task was done. Their immediate desire was the overthrow of Theodore. They hated him and wished to see him dead—but they also feared him greatly. He might not have a very large army left, but he had his guns, and he had his reputation, and they were unlikely to overthrow him themselves. It thus seemed highly desirable that these numerous and well-armed strangers should do the job for them and then go quietly away, leaving the country to be parcelled up between them. They wanted no consul, no interference. One worry was that the British entry into the country might offer some advantage to their great enemies the Egyptians and, as it happened, this was in fact also one of the British worries. In October, the Turkish Viceroy in Egypt had offered mediation, and the British had at first accepted the offer, but when Egyptian troops started massing on the Abyssinian border the whole idea became embarrassing and the offer was rejected. Nothing further was done by Egypt however; her local representatives remained co-operative throughout, but troop movement ceased.

Various chiefs hastily offered support, the most important of them being the ruler of Tigré, the area through which much of the route lay. He had only recently broken away from Theodore and was thus particularly anxious to see him overthrown. As a token of his good faith he attached one of his court officials permanently to the English camp. The individual concerned was a half-caste, the son of an Armenian by an Abyssinian woman, and having been educated in Bombay at a mission school he spoke good English and his advice and assistance proved invaluable. His interest in the overthrow of Theodore was close and personal, for he admitted frankly that if the King were to survive his own life would be forfeit.

General Napier had been careful in his proclamation to deny any wish to interfere with any of the domestic arrangements of the country, (which could be interpreted as meaning that he would not necessarily overthrow Theodore). The chiefs and other leading men, however, took it for granted that this was one of the objects of the expedition, and it seems clear that their subsequent support was offered on that implied understanding.

CHAPTER 6
An Army Assembles

On 2nd January 1868 Sir Robert Napier and his Staff arrived in Annesley Bay. The general had been unwell during the voyage and remained on the ship for a few more days, but by 7th January he was sufficiently recovered to make the sort of landing which the occasion demanded. War might be in the offing, disaster perhaps round the corner, but the formalities had to be observed, so the Commander-in-Chief went ashore in state. Behind him in the bay the seamen of H.M.S. *Octavia*, the warship in which he had travelled, lined the yards while puff after puff of white smoke rolled away from the ship's side as a farewell salute was fired. As his boat approached the jetty the little guns of one of the mountain batteries greeted him in their turn and the General, having inspected a guard of honour of the Kings Own, walked along the jetty and stepped onto African soil.

He was then fifty-eight, a capable, experienced soldier with an excellent record both as a staff officer and a commander. In spite of his position he was a modest, unassuming, approachable man with a pleasant, courteous manner and a beautiful speaking voice; apart from the army and his family, his great love was books—particularly poetry.

He spent the first day or two inspecting the base at Zula and was in general well pleased with what he saw. According to Charles Markham, the geographer who accompanied the expedition and later wrote a full account of it,

He found most of the difficulties overcome and with good reason did he congratulate the advanced force for the progress made in the expedition by the establishment of a firm footing on the highlands of Abyssinia. A desert shore, utterly devoid of resources, had been converted into a very convenient port. After infinite labour the best mountain pass leading to the highlands had been discovered, and the enormous difficulties of making a road up it for cart traffic were nearly overcome. Those intractable robbers, the Shohos, had been turned into carriers, guides, and labourers. An advanced force was encamped on the Abyssinia plateau, and had secured the confidence of the natives; and friendly relations had been established with the great chiefs, up to the very gates of Magdala. The heat and burden of the day were indeed over!

The last sentence was an exaggeration, for a very great deal of work still remained to be done. Nevertheless an excellent start had been made and there was a noticeable air of purpose and activity abroad which augured well for the future. The representatives of the various European armies and navies who had been permitted to accompany the expedition as observers must have been impressed (if, in some cases, a little disappointed) at the order and energy which prevailed everywhere. The crowded shipping, the bursting stores, the neat rows of tethered transport animals, the vast acreage of tents, the railway stretching away across the desert to the foothills, even the flourishing bazaar established for the Indian troops, all indicated a high degree of administrative planning—it was perhaps as well for the reputation of the British Army that its guests had not arrived a few weeks earlier. There were thirteen observers altogether; two Prussians, two Italians, three Frenchmen, two Austrians, two Dutchmen and two Spaniards, and it seems that their presence was not altogether welcome. Captain Hayward wrote in his diary for 25th February:

Brigade field day for the benefit of some "parley-vous" who are out here to pick up what they can. The "Mossieurs" dined at mess this evening and I sat next to one of them, but as I could speak but little French and he less of English, our conversation was not animated.

Various notables also began to assemble; there was the Reverend Krapf—missionary and explorer; Henry Dufton, son of a rich Leeds merchant who had travelled through the country in 1862–3 and had now volunteered his services; Major Grant, who had accompanied Speke on his wanderings to discover the sources of the Nile; Captain Moore, the celebrated Arab traveller; Mr Holmes, from the British Museum, eager for antiquities, and other lesser lights.

The press too was present in considerable force; the *Times*, the *Standard*, the *Morning Post*, the *Daily News*, the *Daily Telegraph*, the *Saturday Review*, and the *Illustrated London News*, the *Times of India* and the *New York Herald* all being represented. Newspaper correspondents were not generally popular on expeditionary forces—the lurid revelations of the Crimea, and to a lesser extent the Mutiny, by the pioneer Russell were too well remembered. The army looked on correspondents with a certain good-natured contempt, although tempered with a respect for their powers. A good press might mean promotion and the Bath, but a poor one could wreck a career, so that ambitious officers tended to handle these strange characters with some circumspection. The younger officers who had little to gain, were not so worried. Young Scott, of the Bengal Artillery, one of Napier's ADCs, put the matter briefly in a letter to his mother:

> We have swarms of special correspondents with us and the general opinion seems to be that we should be much better without them except Dr Austin, the correspondent of the *Times*, who seems an exceedingly nice, gentlemanly man.

The Commander-in-Chief, an eminently reasonable man, knew that the press representatives had a job to do and treated them fairly, neither deferring to them nor ignoring them. He appeared to be well liked and respected by them in return. Mr Shepherd, the special correspondent of the *Times of India* was a particularly gullible individual, and the younger officers of the Headquarters Staff amused themselves by feeding him gravely with the tallest of tall stories, all of which he solemnly sent back to his editor. No record exists of any of them ever actually appear-

ing in the paper, which indicates that the editor was a good deal
more discriminating than his representative.

*   *   *

It was very clear to Napier that his main problem was, and
always would be, the necessity of maintaining a large and highly
efficient transport system, and he bent all his considerable ener-
gies to improving the situation in this respect. It was unfortunate
that so much time had been wasted in Bombay attempting to
concoct a corps on purely Indian lines, but he did what he could
to overcome the more serious defects resulting from the unworkable plans forced on him by the Governor and his Commissariat
advisers.

The immediate requirement was to establish considerable
dumps of supplies at Senafé, and the best answer seemed to be
to make the road passable for wheeled traffic. This was not
as difficult as it first appeared since, with the exception of one
or two bad places, the path rose remarkably evenly at a gradient
of about one in forty—well within the capacity of a fully laden
Indian bullock cart. More and more soldiers were therefore set
to navvying, and at the end of January the first convoy of
seventy-five carts trundled safely onto the plateau. The improvement was immediate, for while a pack animal might carry at
most a hundred and forty pounds of stores, plus its forage,
a pair in draught could haul six or seven hundredweight quite
comfortably on the existing gradients. The discovery of large
quantities of good grass in some of the side valleys along the
route helped matters still more by doing away with the need
for animals to carry their own fodder with them.

In spite of this improvement, it soon became clear to Napier
that his original plan of establishing sufficient dumps of food to
make his force independent of local supply was not feasible. It
could of course be done, given time, but in this case time meant
a probable minimum of eighteen months, and it was absolutely
certain that the British Government would not tolerate this sort of
delay. Expense and public opinion alike would make it unthinkable. He thus decided that as a matter of necessity he would

be compelled to rely to some extent on local supply and local transport, both of which were fortunately working well.

Until the arrival of General Staveley the losses of transport animals through starvation, thirst, disease, and general neglect had been enormous. Out of some eight thousand beasts landed, no more than five and a half thousand had survived, and many of these, weakened by their earlier privations, were in no real state to work. They were driven, dragged, and flogged along as a matter of hard necessity, but the carcases littering the sides of the track up the pass told their own grim story. Fresh animals continued to arrive, and proper arrangements for food, water, and veterinary services ensured that losses amongst these new-comers were kept reasonably low. By the end of February nearly six thousand more had been landed; the bulk were mules, but there were also large numbers of horses, ponies, bullocks, and camels.

Large quantities of transport equipment had also arrived but a surprising amount of it proved useless. It appeared, for ex-ample, that no one had ever previously invented a suitable mili-tary packsaddle for use in the British service. Whole shiploads of saddles arrived, many apparently designed by people who had never seen a mule. Charles Markham, who had had a good deal of assorted experience with the breed during his travels in South America described one saddle as being "a structure between a hatchway ladder and a hencoop". These strange saddles not only galled the unfortunate beasts cruelly but also made it impossible for the inexperienced muleteers to fasten their loads securely. They slipped backwards uphill, forwards downhill, and all ways on the level, often bringing down the weakened beasts with them.

Markham advocated the Spanish *aparejo* which consisted of two tightly stuffed leather cushions fastened along one edge. The cushions rested on the back muscles in an inverted V, leaving the spine clear, and were held securely in place by a girth. Count Kodolitsch, one of the Austrian observers who had seen much service in Mexico, made the same recommendation but nothing came of it, largely because there was no time.

The most useless of the original muleteers had been sacked

(over four thousand having been sent back to Egypt alone), but in many cases the sufferings they had imposed by sheer cruelty were replaced by equal suffering born of ignorance. The Transport Corps learnt its business as it went along, and many thousand unfortunate beasts died in the process.

Things improved slowly. The volunteer officers running the Corps sweated and slaved and swore, and slowly a workable organization was hammered out. The corps was organized into lettered divisions of two thousand animals, consisting as far as possible, of one species only. A division was commanded by a captain assisted by two subalterns, together with four inspectors, twenty troop sergeants, and eighty sergeants, almost all drawn from various British and Indian Regiments; it also included twenty-three smiths and farriers, and most important of all— six hundred and sixty-seven muleteers.

After allowing for sickness, this establishment meant that each muleteer had to be responsible for three or four animals, which was found in practice to be unworkable. The mules were often unbroken and it might take an inexperienced man hours to load his charges. It also meant that mules had to be tethered nose to tail in fours and dragged along, a thoroughly inefficient way of doing things. Even the best beasts could hardly keep their balance when subjected to violent, unexpected jerks from their neighbours, and when they fell it often happened that they could not get up. Mules go better either unattached after a leader or when led singly, and this was eventually realized. Later, on long marches, mules for which there were no muleteers were led by infantrymen, and although this naturally reduced the fighting efficiency of the battalions it correspondingly accelerated movement and reduced casualties.

The most fortunate beasts, initially at any rate, were the forty-four elephants. They were government animals which had come from India with their mahouts and adequate supplies of their accustomed diet, so that they did not suffer in the same way as the other species. They were, however, surprisingly delicate animals and lack of shelter, lack of sleep, even bird droppings on their fodder, were liable to make them ill. Extremes of temperature and altitude and hard work did eventually take their toll and not all survived to return to Bombay. They had originally been included in the expedition mainly to carry the Armstrong guns should the tracks prove too bad for draft, but they were also used to some extent for general transport purposes.

It was the presence of elephants with the force which impressed the Abyssinians more than anything else; they were familiar with elephants which were wild, untameable beasts, given to savage charges when provoked. They were astounded to see elephants tamed and handled by man.

The various Shohos employed as labourers at the base were at first terrified, and would run off in panic if an elephant flicked its trunk at a fly, but later they became braver, and eventually managed to help load them with great *sang-froid*.

The last, and by far the most modern form of transport was the railway. The worst part of the whole route to Magdala was the first few miles across the salt desert, and a line across that strip was highly desirable. Skilled labour was scarce, and as wells had to be dug to provide water at regular intervals, progress was slow. Fortunately the arrival in December 1867 of an Army Works Corps, enlisted for general labour duties under the Royal Engineers, helped things considerably, particularly since it included in its ranks a number of Chinese with some experience of railway construction. Early in 1868 a further welcome increase in the labour force was the arrival of a coolie corps.

*   *   *

Tactical planning for the campaign rested entirely on the transport situation. It seemed clear that in material terms Theodore's power was almost gone, and that apart from his reputation (which naturally impressed the local chiefs more than it did the British), he was no more than a guerrilla leader with six or seven thousand men and a considerable train of guns and mortars of various calibres, some very large. But even these guns were probably an encumbrance. Theodore loved artillery for its own sake—guns were a symbol of power to every Abyssinian—but it was unlikely that he had any gunners who were

91

capable of handling them with any real effect except at point blank ranges.

On the purely military side therefore the odds were with the British. Every man's hand was against the King; his army was dwindling rapidly from desertion, and he was surrounded by enemies only waiting the opportunity to pull him down. The most dangerous of his enemies were the British and for that reason, and for that reason only, the Abyssinians were pro-British—but this could change. A reverse, even a slight one, could restore Theodore's reputation of invincibility and bring the whole pack down on Napier's force, partly for the arms and other loot, and partly to be on the winning side. If this happened, the British chances of fighting their way back down the defiles might be small; the Kabul disaster of 1842 was still comparatively fresh in the minds of all Indian soldiers of any seniority, and no one wanted a similar reverse in Africa.

One important factor continued to be the safety of the prisoners, for whose sake the whole vast effort was being made. They were at Magdala, while Theodore was far off to the west, but reputedly he had set out from Debra Tabor and was moving slowly through a rugged and hostile country, encumbered with followers and guns, on his painful way back to his last stronghold.

At his reported rate of progress it would take him weeks to get there; indeed letters from the prisoners were almost unanimous in their opinion that he would never reach Magdala at all unless he abandoned his guns—in which case he could be there in a few days.

There was at the time a strong feeling (not in Abyssinia) that what was required was a bold dash by a few hundred light horsemen who would burst into Magdala and snatch away the prisoners before Theodore arrived there. The Duke of Cambridge, writing from Horse Guards on 18th February, told Napier:

> What is much desired here is that a flying column or a succession of flying columns should be pushed forward and operate to the front, so as to make a dash if possible and finish the business before the rains set in.

General Napier, needless to say, had considered the idea too, but had rejected it for the club armchair strategy that it was. On an open, well-watered plain it might have been attractive, but to send such a force blundering across mountains and ravines would be to court disaster. Nobody who served with the Abyssinian expedition ever doubted this. Doctor Blanc did indeed suggest that a flying column of eight hundred cavalry, three hundred European infantry mounted on mules, and four guns, would be a sufficient force to release him and his fellow captives but he was hardly an impartial authority.

Towards the end of January, Napier considered that the time had come when he could begin pushing troops forward in a careful and methodical way. He had done all that he could do at Zula and was understandably anxious to see what conditions were like on the plateau. He therefore dispatched a warning order to General Collings at Senafé to be prepared to move forward. On 25th January he set off up the pass.

Before leaving Napier invited the Senior Naval Officer to provide a small naval brigade from the warships in Annesley Bay to accompany his force to Magdala. The Royal Navy had seconded him magnificently at Zula and he wished to show his gratitude in the most popular way possible. The offer was accepted with celerity; a small force of some ninety bluejackets was quickly organized under Captain Fellowes of H.M.S. *Dryad*, and equipped as a rocket brigade. The rocket had had a somewhat chequered career. It was erratic and inaccurate, but it had the great advantage that it could be fired from a light tube which could easily be transported to places where guns could not go, so it seemed suitable for Abyssinia. The brigade had twelve tubes and a thousand six-pounder Hales rockets, the rank and file also being armed with Snider carbines and cutlasses.

The General travelled lightly, accompanied only by his son Robert (one of his ADCs). Captain Scott, the second ADC, was left to bring on the spare horses, the baggage, and the servants. Napier, conscious that he should set an example of economy in transport, ordered that his baggage should be restricted to three mule loads, but young Scott, like any good ADC, had anticipated this and had taken the precaution of hiring a party of country camels and sending them on up the pass in advance, laden with beer, brandy, port, and various tinned foods. The General was inclined to be generous with his invitations to dine, and his ADC, who amongst his other duties was responsible for the catering, did not propose to be caught out. Ration beef, chupattis and a dram of rum and water might be honest camp fare, but hospitality and prestige alike demanded that something a little better should be laid before the guests of the Commander-in-Chief, for as long as possible.

Napier's first stage was to Kumayli at the foot of the pass, a dull, hot, uncomfortable ride across fourteen miles of burning salt desert along a track marked by the rotting carcases of transport animals, each with its obscene cluster of vultures. He inspected the camp closely and next morning went on up the pass. The path followed a dry torrent bed, and as it rose higher up the pass the cliffs closed in threateningly, until twelve miles further on at Suru they were hundreds of feet high and no more than a few yards apart. Here Napier stopped to inspect and approve the elevated path raised over the jumbled boulders by the Indian sappers; here too there was running water, fresh and clean but hot to the touch. Two miles further on he reached the camp at upper Suru, which had been selected because of its good water. An excellent spring bubbled out of the rocks, and below it half a dozen barrels had been sunk into the ground to provide clean and convenient watering places for the animals.

The General's son was taken ill at Suru and his father decided to leave him behind in the capable hands of the Medical Officer of the Baluchis who were busy road-building in the vicinity. The doctor was something of a character, and apart from his medical abilities had recently established a reputation as a big game shot. He had been out a few days previously, reconnoitring a new water point in a side valley when he had come unexpectedly on five elephants, grazing peacefully, and had at once stalked and shot two of them with no more concern than if they had been rabbits. Two other officers of the regiment had been less lucky. Fired by his example they too had gone elephant hunting, and having found a small herd (possibly the survivors of the Doctor's *battue*), had selected a likely beast and both fired at it from behind, upon which the irritated animal at once swung round and charged them. One was badly gored before the other succeeded in killing the beast.

On 27th January a long, dull pull of thirteen miles brought the General to his next night's staging point at Undul Wells. Here the water was brought to the surface by the most modern pattern American pump. From Undul Wells Napier rode on across the Guineafowl Plain—so christened by the reconnaissance party—and on to Rara Gudi in a hollow in the hills. Next morning a steep pull up of some three thousand feet in eight miles finally brought him to Senafé, on the edge of the plateau and sixty-six miles from the coast. He must have felt that at last he was making progress, although there was still a long way to go.

Senafé was quite a pleasant place, and having been garrisoned for some time it had a reasonably settled appearance. A mixture of strict discipline and generous payment had reconciled the locals to the presence of the troops, so that a market had been opened and a certain amount of local produce, mostly grain and forage, was available for purchase by the Commissariat department. The people, who seemed wretchedly poor, also brought in firewood and water to sell to the Indian soldiers. They had learnt the Indian words for them and their cries of "lakri" and "pani" could be heard round the lines far into the night. It is not clear what currency was used, for the troops can hardly have been flush with dollars.

Senafé was some eight thousand feet above sea level and the climate was pleasant. It was, however, extremely cold at night—often below freezing point—so that blankets and warm clothing were essential. This had been foreseen and provision made for it, but it nevertheless threw a considerable extra strain onto the already overworked transport. The troops usually carried a blanket, a greatcoat, and a waterproof sheet with them, but they could hardly be expected to carry more, and everything else had to go by mule.

Understandably there was not a great deal for the troops to do in their leisure time. The food, although adequate and wholesome, was dull; the European rations consisted of a pound and

a quarter of meat, bread, flour, or biscuit as available, compressed vegetables, tea and sugar. Rum was included in the daily
ration, but there was no other drink available. The native rations
often presented a greater transport problem than those of the
Europeans. Most Indians ate little or no meat, so that much of
their food—rice and similar bulk cereals—had to be carried in,
while the British beef was usually purchased locally on the hoof
and marched with the columns until required.

Work minimized boredom, but the troops were nevertheless
beginning to look forward to an advance and some fighting as
a change from road-building.

Shooting was a popular pastime with the officers, not only for
the sport but also because almost anything made a welcome
change from tough beef. There was quite a lot of game about;
hares were particularly plentiful for the locals apparently dis-
dained them as unclean. The troops killed them by the hundred
with sticks, sometimes actually among the tents. There were also
guineafowl and francolin in fair numbers, together with a few
antelope. Young Ensign Wynter of the 33rd, road-making with
his company a few miles further south, was out every evening
with a pin-fire gun; cartridges for it were in short supply, and as
he was shooting primarily for the pot he made it a practice as
far as possible to get half a dozen birds in line before he fired.
Not at all the thing at an English covert shoot, but an excellent
way of supplementing rations in the Abyssinian wilderness.

It was at this time that the 33rd Regiment lost its commanding
officer as the result of a shooting accident. Alexander Dunn had
been a colourful character with a variety of military experience.
He first purchased a commission in the 11th Hussars in 1852 at
the age of twenty, and took part in the famous Light Brigade
charge at Balaclava, where he was the only officer to receive the
Victoria Cross. After the Crimean War he sold out and went
to Canada where his father was Receiver-General. There he
helped to raise the Royal Canadians, a regiment composed of
colonists of British descent who were anxious to serve their
mother-country, and which was later taken onto the British
establishment as the 100th Foot. Dunn commanded this regiment
for a while before exchanging into the 33rd in 1864.

10 General Sir Robert Napier, KCB, GSCI, Commander of the Abyssinian Expedition. *(Illustrated London News)*

11 Captain Charles Speedy, one of the most enigmatic figures of the expedition, in Abyssinian native dress. *(Army Museums Ogilby Trust)*

12   The Devil's Staircase at Suru, showing how difficult the
terrain proved for the advance column in their road clearing and
construction capacity. *(National Army Museum)*

13   Looking down from Magdala to the countryside over which
the expedition made their approach march. *(Stephen Bell &
John Fynn)*

14   Some of Theodore's European artisans; the men who built
the artillery in which he so firmly believed. *(Army Museums
Ogilby Trust)*

15   A group photograph showing some of the missionaries after
their release by Theodore; some still with the shackles which had
bound them for so long. *(Army Museum Ogilby Trust)*

16 A pen and water-colour sketch of the final assault on the fortress of Magdala. The infantry are advancing in line, while rockets from the Naval battery may be seen passing overhead. (*Army Museums Ogilby Trust*)

17 Magdala today—a recent photograph. (*Stephen Bell & John Fynn*)

18 Brigadier-General Merewether with Prince Kasai's envoy. Monsieur Murizinger is seated on the General's other side; the European sitting cross-legged is Captain Speedy. (*National Army Museum*)

According to young Scott's description of the accident, Colonel Dunn was,

> Leaning over going uphill to take some water from his servant below him; he leant his arm, it appears, over the muzzle of his rifle, and his gaiter or something or other caught in the trigger, sending the contents of both barrels through his body, one of the barrels being loaded with slugs. He was greatly liked by his men and everybody, being a most popular man, and had just got command of his Regiment for the campaign.

He was barely thirty-five at the time of his death, tall handsome, good natured, and something of a dandy. Young Wynter said roundly that he was a "bad Commanding Officer and not a good example to young officers" and that "although a popular man he had gone far to destroy the Regiment". Young officers often tend to be censorious but in this case there might have been something in what he said for the 33rd was a hard-case regiment and had perhaps needed a firmer hand than their commanding officer considered necessary. Command of the 33rd was taken over by Cooper, the senior major, who having spent much of his time on the staff was little known to the regiment.

General Napier had several conversations at Senafé with Merewether, who had by now been promoted Brigadier-General and appointed Political Officer to the expedition. Merewether had been ranging far south and his firm opinion was that the people were, and would remain, friendly. His only fear was that the Egyptians might try to take advantage of any confusion caused by the British entry into Abyssinia to improve their own situation. He had good grounds for his apprehensions, but diplomatic pressure by the British on the rulers of Egypt prevented any incidents.

In view of Merewether's confidence in the situation in the country the Commander-in-Chief decided to continue his slow advance southward, and on 2nd February he despatched Merewether to Adigrat, forty miles further south, accompanied by Brigadier-General Collings with half the 33rd Regiment, and a battalion of native infantry. Troops in the rear all then moved one stage forward.

It was all very slow and cautious—not a bit like the swift, audacious dash of light horsemen envisaged in the London clubs. But it seemed to be working. The transport corps stood the strain, the track improved daily, the locals remained friendly. Napier was doing no more than flex his muscles and shift his feet; when all was ready he would lunge.

CHAPTER 7

The March Begins

CAPTAIN SPEEDY joined the Headquarters at Senafé. Since leaving Abyssinia he had been farming in New Zealand and had commanded a militia company in the second Maori war. The home authorities, thinking that his previous experience in the country would prove useful, had summoned him back, and he had responded at once. On arrival at Zula he borrowed a horse and rode off southwards in case his services were required, leaving his baggage to follow on in the care of a couple of hastily hired Shohos, He thus arrived in Senafé with no more than the clothes he stood in, but he seemed content with this situation and having borrowed a few essentials soon made himself at home. He had no tent and so slept in a *dooli*, an enclosed Indian stretcher usually used for transporting wounded. His enormous rawboned frame, spade beard, and thick glasses were soon familiar sights about the camp; he was by all accounts a pleasant, likeable man, not a bit the swashbuckling desperado some people had expected, and quickly became popular. He spoke Amharic well and soon made himself useful in many ways.

On 4th February the headquarters moved south to Adigrat— an unprepossessing, tumbledown village, its only place of interest being a church. Much of the interior walls of the building was adorned with primitive but striking murals of biblical scenes; the painting which most amused the irreverent soldiers was the one depicting the Israelites crossing the Red Sea, each man holding a matchlock musket high above his head to keep

99

the charge dry. The "bells" of the church were in fact two pieces of a peculiar type of rock suspended from a tree by leather thongs, which when struck with a padded stick gave out deep, bell-like notes.

Headquarters were followed by the 4th Regiment, the Baluchis, a British sapper company, and the battery of Armstrong guns. Napier's ADC, watching the Kings Own march in, thought what

> a fine lot of fellows they looked in their Kharker [*sic*] clothing, and beards covered in dust; they stepped out as fresh at the end of their march as if they were just starting . . . not a single straggler and the hospital tent empty.

The guns, which had been driven the whole way, created a sensation amongst the locals. Guns were power in Abyssinia and the presence of these shining monsters, each drawn by its smart team of eight greys, did much to convince them that Theodore's time was come. It had not been easy to get them so far in draught; the track had proved to be very bad, and in some places it had been necessary to take the teams out and haul the guns along by manpower, with hundreds of sweating infantrymen on the drag ropes. Descents were sometimes as bad as up slopes. Often it was possible to lock the wheels and get the guns down them with the powerful wheelers only, but once or twice the guns ran away and on one occasion a horse was killed when a piece went over a cliff. Fortunately the battery was accompanied by two elephants and these succeeded in getting the gun back onto the path. The elephants created a sensation in Adigrat as they had done all along the route.

The people in Adigrat were true Abyssinians, dark-skinned but with sharp, non-negroid features. Their usual dress was a white waistcloth or drawers and a wide, loose cloak of some linen material, rarely very clean. Their hair was twisted into strange shapes and dressed liberally with butter which, coupled with the fact that they rarely washed, gave them a characteristic rancid smell. The Christians, who were in the great majority, denoted their adherence to the true faith by wearing a piece of blue cord or ribbon round their necks, from which was often suspended a small copper earscoop. Every man carried a curved sword, usually sharpened on the inner edge like a sickle, a stick or spear, and a round leather shield.

The women, kept very much in their place, were in general unattractive. A few of the young ones were quite pretty but were usually caked with dirt and grease, as were the leather petticoats which constituted their sole garments.

The climate at Adigrat was mild and the soil fertile, and for the first time the expedition began to see patches of cultivation, mostly small fields of unripe barley. Grass was also plentiful which eased the Commissariat's difficulties, although their problems continued to be enormous. At one stage indeed it was proposed to Napier that the forward troops should be put on half-rations, but this he refused to do; the men were doing a great deal of hard physical work on the track and he considered it essential that they should continue to be well fed at all costs. The provision of human food alone required a hundred and seventy mule loads daily, to say nothing of grass for the animals, and there were also tents, hospital supplies, reserve ammunition, warm clothing and money to be carried. The latter in particular proved a constant strain on the transport, for one animal could only carry between fifteen hundred and two thousand dollars and the daily requirement was enormous. The dollars did not circulate in the accepted sense, since there were no banks or other means of recovering the money in exchange for cheques or paper. The coins were simply paid over to the locals who promptly hoarded them away and hurried back for more.

One solution to the problem of supply was to reduce the number of useless mouths, of which initially there were hundreds. An Anglo-Indian army trailed along servants and followers in vast numbers and although they might be justified on the hot plains of India the bulk of them were quite unnecessary in the temperate Abyssinian highlands. Their numbers were thinned out ruthlessly, and a steady stream of Indian non-combatants began moving back to Zula to the great benefit of the overworked transport corps. Unit stores were also overhauled at the same time and considerable quantities of surplus items placed in dumps.

A further improvement in transport arrangements was made by reorganizing the corps into two separate sections. The best animals and muleteers (including the excellent trains from Bengal) were named the highland division and were designated for work from Adigrat southwards, while the other, the lowland division, operated back to Zula. Local transport by contract was still encouraged, and a great deal of useful work was done by the Abyssinians. Much of their co-operation was due to the unremitting activities of the political officers attached to the Force. Major Grant had done particularly well at Adowa as Napier's representative at the court of the Prince of Tigré. Grant's presence had pleased and flattered the latter and ensured his continued goodwill, and as much of the route lay through territory over which he claimed suzerainty, this was important.

General Merewether also continued his local work, with great success. Strict discipline and fair dealing were the secrets of success along the route, and although the locals were at first inclined to be wary, the plentiful supply of silver soon dispersed their fears. The real problem was not lack of willingness to sell, but simply the lack of available surpluses. The natives ate little meat, relying chiefly on cereals; the main item of diet was *tef* bread made from one of the numerous cereals available. A combination of drought and locusts, however, had reduced their grain supplies to near starvation level, and although they caught, fried, and ate locusts in large numbers—an appropriate enough vengeance—this did not compensate for lack of cereal.

Far ahead of the force ranged the Quartermaster-General with his pioneer force of a hundred and fifty sabres, two companies of native infantry, a company of Punjab Pioneers, and a company of Bombay sappers. Colonel Phayre was in his element, exploring largely unknown country, scrambling for miles over broken, rocky passes, sketching, mapping, and patching up the track as he went. The Abyssinians called him the *Fitaurari*—their word for an Advanced Guard Commander, and a title which blended euphoniously with his own surname. The area was completely unsurveyed so that anyone leaving the well marked main route had to rely on such rough maps as could be produced by Phayre and other staff officers. One very modern feature of the campaign was that the force included a photographic detachment of Royal Engineers whose main task was to reproduce these maps in some quantities. It was a technique which had been used extensively in the later days of the American Civil War, but was still a novelty outside the United States. The detachment also recorded scenes of local interest including several inevitable group photographs of British and Abyssinian dignitaries.

By 15th February he was in Antalo, about ninety miles further south, and Brigadier-General Collings at once set off to support him with a wing of the 33rd, a European mountain battery, and a squadron of the Sind Horse. They found that the path was not quite as good as Phayre's rather optimistic reports had suggested, and a few mules were lost *en route*. The march was dreary, much of it over a wide, rocky plain, but at least there were adequate supplies of water.

Behind the headquarters a detachment of British engineers were working hard to get a telegraph line forward, and by mid-February it had reached Senafé. The main problem proved to be the provision of poles; in the passes the insulators were fixed to rocks, but it was difficult to find suitable timber amongst the stunted trees on the plateau, nor could poles be carried up from the coast. This problem, like a number of others, was solved by the resourceful Speedy, who started local purchase on generous terms. The word soon went round that the mad strangers were offering dollars for poles, and the locals came swarming in with them. In their anxiety not to miss their share of the silver harvest, many of the villagers unroofed their own houses.

The Prince of Tigré had expressed a wish to meet Napier and after many delays this was finally arranged. The difficulties were caused by the Prince, who having only recently seized power in the province was understandably apprehensive of being overthrown by some rival as soon as his back was turned. Eventually, due mainly to the tact and diplomacy of Major Grant and Captain Speedy, the meeting was finally arranged and on 25th February General Napier moved off with a small escort of about five hundred men to meet the dilatory ruler at the place agreed.

The British troops established themselves on one side of a

103

shallow valley through which ran a stream, the other side being left free for the Abyssinians, and after a wait of two or three hours the Prince appeared with his army, an apparently well-disciplined force of some four thousand men. A red tent—the traditional Abyssinian sign of royalty—was pitched for him on the crest of the slope and there he rested for a time. His army then formed up in line and advanced towards the stream to the rattling of crude kettledrums; Prince Kasai rode behind the centre, his position being marked by red and yellow flags, and a hundred yards short of the watercourse he halted his army and awaited the approach of Napier.

The British advanced in silence, General Napier riding on an elephant to the astonishment and admiration of the Abyssinians. The approach of the great beast unfortunately worried the Tigréan horses so much that the British Commander-in-Chief, not wishing to cause a panic, prudently dismounted and rode the rest of the way on a charger, flanked by his staff. As he neared the stream a gap opened in the centre of the line opposite him and Prince Kasai also rode forward on a richly caprisoned white mule, a great scarlet umbrella being borne over him.

The two dismounted and shook hands, then Napier conducted the Prince to a tent which had been pitched by the stream. As he did so the British guard of honour fired a *feu-de-joie* which set all the Abyssinian mules and horses kicking and plunging and caused some confusion in the opposing camp. The Abyssinians had a tendency to wince at loud bangs, since unexpected bursts of fire meant one thing to them—treachery; but seeing the muzzles of the rifles pointing in the air reassured them, so that when the battery began in its turn to fire a salute they were able to retain their composure.

The meeting, as to be expected, was tedious in the extreme. After numerous compliments from both sides Kasai made it clear that he loved the English, hated Theodore, and fully intended—come what may—to continue as ruler of Tigré. He then suggested delicately that he would appreciate some assistance in dealing with certain rivals, and that in particular a gift of arms would be most welcome, a request which Napier tactfully managed to shelve. Eternal friendship was then sworn and Sir Robert presented the Prince with a very fine double-barrelled rifle and some glassware as presents from his Queen, together with a personal gift from himself—the charger he had ridden to the interview. At least that was the intention, but his ADC had other ideas:

> Sir Robert also presented him with the horse he had ridden over to meet him. I grudged very much having to hand him over, but it was arranged beforehand. It was a horse I had bought for Sir Robert in Bombay, just before leaving, as an extra charger if necessary. I bought a batch of three in that way, and he was the best of the lot. I slipped out, had the saddle and bridle put on another horse, and got *him* ready for presentation!

Shortage of supplies made alcohol scarce, but the medical comforts box yielded up a bottle of port and another of brandy so that modest hospitality could be dispensed. It was speedily consumed from the presentation goblets, and according to Abyssinian custom General Napier drank first to prove that it was not poisoned. One of his staff, a Household cavalryman, remarked cynically that from his experience of hospital port the precaution was not altogether an unnecessary one.

When the drinks were finished (which did not take long), a group photograph was taken by the engineers, after which a few selected chiefs were allowed to ride—with some trepidation —on the elephant, Kasai meanwhile, made his first close acquaintance with the tactics and equipment of a modern army. He watched with interest while the cavalry charged and the infantry skirmished and formed square, but the things which really impressed him were the guns, which he inspected carefully, handling the shells and peering down the rifled barrels.

Some of his followers were heard to remark with great seriousness that the English must be good Christians or heaven would not grant them the intelligence to make such splendid weapons. Captain Hozier, the assistant military secretary, commented disapprovingly,

> It appeared that to their view the greatest blessings which could be vouchsafed to Christian morality are firearms and gunpowder.

A belief not held exclusively by Abyssinians.

Prince Kasai then became host in his turn, and invited the General and his staff to his tent across the valley. As they rode forward, the Tigréan army, which had been squatting in line, motionless and silent during the whole meeting, rose to its feet and swarmed round them, so that Scott momentarily suspected treason in his turn and began to calculate what chance he would have to use his sabre before being pulled down. Fortunately the matter was never put to the test. In the tent they all sat on the ground and were entertained by wild music played on pipes. Refreshments were then served, consisting of baskets of spongy *tef* bread with bowls of liquid curry into which it was first dunked, together with numerous flasks of *tej*, a mead-like drink made of honey and flavoured with herbs.

As the party broke up the Prince presented Napier with a lion-skin cloak, a spear, a sword, one of the silver-gilt armlets usually given as a reward for gallantry in battle, and, finally, with his white mule. The General rode back to camp on it in all his finery, although it was then too dark for his own soldiers to appreciate the spectacle. Napier's ADC, writing to his mother later, commented dryly that under all its splendid trappings the mule had a very sore back.

Next morning there was a further meeting, brief, unofficial and less spectacular, but very useful. In the course of it Kasai promised to supply considerable quantities of grain at various depots along the road, a promise which was faithfully kept.

They then parted and on the same day the British moved on to Antalo. The march was arduous, for little work had been done on the track and progress was correspondingly slow. The Armstrong guns had a particularly difficult time for the path was unsuited to wheels and the splendid teams were beginning to show the effects of their previous efforts. The guns had to be manhandled for much of the way by the infantry, but even with the greatest care and hundreds of men on the ropes one gun ran off the road and broke a wheel. Fortunately, as before, the elephants were able to recover it, but it was clear that further accidents were to be anticipated. It was as a result of the experiences on this march that Napier decided that from Antalo onwards the guns were to be carried by elephants.

Hundreds of pack animals were lost on this stretch. Those which broke their legs or otherwise injured themselves in falls were destroyed, but those which collapsed from exhaustion were simply left. There was water and grazing along the route, and it was hoped that some at least might recover.

Further south Colonel Phayre found the track very poor and his party spent so much time road-building that they were finding it difficult to keep ahead of the main body. At one point they were given false information by a petty chief who was not anxious for the road to pass close to his *amba*, with the result that a whole week's work was wasted on a stretch of path which was never in fact used. In order to give the locals some warning of their approach, M. Munzinger rode on ahead of the reconnaissance party with half a dozen men to establish contact with the various chiefs along the way.

Napier reached Antalo on 2nd March and decided to halt there for a few days. The delay was forced on him partly to allow Phayre time to get ahead, partly to allow some essential troops—including the 45th Regiment and a wing of the 3rd Dragoon Guards—to catch up, and partly because the force was running short of currency—the vital dollars on which all else depended. During this period Antalo, the intended advance base, was put into a state of defence. Napier did not anticipate any interference during his advance but he had had enough experience of warfare in Asia to realize the almost irresistible urge which primitive people had to harry a withdrawing force. Antalo was well situated in that it covered the main approaches to Galla country.

Antalo was the furthest point reached by the telegraph, which proved invaluable. So popular was it—not always for strictly essential purposes—that its use was eventually restricted to unit commanders and officers of the QMG's staff. Other communications—messages and mail—were carried by small detachments of Indian cavalry established along the full length of the route.

By the time Antalo was reached baggage had been cut drastically. Officers were restricted to a mule between two, and soldiers were allowed twenty-five pounds of baggage, including their bedding. Followers too had almost disappeared, which effected a surprising saving in transport for most of them did not eat meat and had needed a considerable bulk of cereal foods, much of which had to be carried up from the coast. They were also particularly susceptible to the cold and so needed a good deal of warm clothing and bedding.

After a ten-day halt at Antalo the advance continued, but it was a slow and painful business. The tracks were bad, the mountains high and steep, and the pack animals weakened visibly. Even the troops were beginning to show signs of exhaustion, for although their bedding was carried for them they were still heavily laden with arms, equipment, food, and water, and the constant climbing was beginning to have its effect. When an officer of the 33rd explained to his section that they were on a tableland, one of his soldiers replied with Irish humour that the table was upside down and they were climbing the legs, a comment with which most of the infantry would have heartily agreed.

At Antalo the Commander-in-Chief had divided his force into two divisions, the first of which was to carry on southwards while the second comprised all the troops on the lines of communication. Sir Charles Staveley, who had finally handed over Zula and hurried forward, took over command of the first Division, and immediately ordered that no more than one mule was to be led by one man. This he achieved by detailing infantrymen as mule leaders, and the improvement was immediate. The animals were able to pick their way over rough places without constantly being toppled by the mules on either side, and casualties from falls were appreciably reduced. The system increased the work of the infantry somewhat but it seemed on balance that they had more reserve strength than the mules; and so it proved. The system also meant that battalions were less combat ready on the march, but this was considered an acceptable risk. The attitude of the locals made it clear that they were unlikely to become aggressors, and Theodore, the real enemy, was still far off to the south-west.

On 18th March the main body, which was now close behind Phayre's reconnaissance party, reached Lake Ashangi, approached by a narrow irregular path winding round a heavily forested spur. The lake itself was beautifully situated in a hollow in the hills and surrounded by field after field of growing corn. The place abounded in geese, and those sportsmen who had had both the foresight and the hardihood to haul their shotguns so far had excellent sport and a change of diet. One enterprising officer actually succeeded in killing a goose with his revolver although it is not clear whether this was due to the excellence of his shooting or the *naïvetté* of his quarry. The borders of the lake were extremely swampy and one or two unwary wild fowlers had narrow escapes from the apparently bottomless mud.

Mr Shepherd (the *Times of India* special correspondent) later wrote a book on the expedition in which he related a story that a raiding party of some three hundred mounted Gallas had been driven into the swamp only a few weeks before by a superior force of Abyssinians, and had all disappeared. Although possible, one is rather driven to conclude that this may have been one of the unlikely stories with which the young Headquarters officers were wont to regale him.

At Lake Ashangi the 33rd Regiment actually had a full parade, the first for many weeks and thus something of a change from the steady pick and shovel work which had been their lot for some time past. The sound of the band, and particularly the appearance of the troops in scarlet instead of the drab khaki to which the locals had become accustomed, quickly drew admiring crowds from the neighbouring villages.

Here too, various letters came in from the prisoners, although they told Napier little that he did not know. It seemed to be amply confirmed that Theodore was still making his slow way towards Magdala and was by then very close. One noticeable theme in almost all these letters was their unwilling admiration for the persistence shown by the King—to whom they always referred as "Bob"—and their admission that he would after all get his guns to their destination. The prisoners were clearly, and understandably, apprehensive of what their treatment would be when Theodore finally arrived. Doctor Blanc, urging haste, wrote,

In the meanwhile delay may be death. I know you are doing your best, so trust in you and God that all may be

well. If not, never mind, only polish off as many of Bob's
vagabonds as you can.

The leading troops reached Lat on 22nd March, and there
Napier halted to make his final preparations for the last lap
to Magdala. The scale of stores was again reduced; tents were
still carried for health reasons, but on a scale of one to twelve
officers or twenty men, with a very few extra for the staff and for
hospital use. All sick—human and animals—were left behind.
Officers were allowed private pack animals but their loads were
limited to bedding. No mule was to carry more than a hundred
pounds, and each was to be led individually. Rations were reduced to flour, dried vegetables, tea, and a little rum, plus of
course bullocks on the hoof.

The troops marched in either red serge or drill, according to
orders issued by the brigades, the suit not worn being carried.
This caused some transport problems but was unavoidable because
of the wide temperature variations between day and night. The
men wore the normal equipment of cartridge box and sling, belt
and bayonet, and haversack and water bottle, with of course,
their rifles, and at least one British battalion wore an extra small
pouch on the belt containing a further ten rounds of ammunition. Knapsacks were not carried but the blanket or greatcoat
rolled in the waterproof sheet was tied into a loop and worn
over one shoulder, pioneer fashion. Altogether the individual
soldier carried something over fifty pounds on his back.

The general appearance of the British troops had deteriorated;
their clothing was beginning to show signs of wear and this,
combined with the beards that most of them were wearing, gave
them a piratical appearance which it is to be feared the soldiers
rather cultivated. Times were changing and the days of immacu-
late scarlet were numbered. The beau ideal of a soldier—
fostered by the Mutiny—had become a bronzed, bearded individual, preferably in a funny hat and tattered drill stained with
coffee. Boots and socks gave a good deal of trouble, for most
of the troops wore Indian-made footgear which was considerably
inferior to the British ammunition boot, and the Bombay-made
socks had a stitched seam down the back which caused sores.

An extra, free issue of boots was eventually made to all troops who went south of Antalo.

It was particularly noticeable that the appearance of the Indian troops did not deteriorate to the same extent as that of the British, and although their clothes gradually wore out, their officers seem to have insisted to the very end on a high standard of cleanliness and neatness.

From Lat onwards the first division was organized into three brigades, two to move ahead and the third, a temporary one composed chiefly of sappers and pioneers, to follow close behind, improving the road as it went. It was also to guard the dumps at Lat and to be responsible for facilitating as far as possible the movement of other troops called forward by Napier.

CHAPTER 8
The King Moves East

THEODORE, who by now was indubitably mad, continued to rage across the country round Debra Tabor, burning and killing in a wild, senseless orgy of destruction and death.

Flad, who had been the bearer of the letter to England demanding artisans, reached Theodore in April 1867 with England's firm refusal, together with a clear threat that continued detention of the prisoners would have the most serious consequences for their captor. It must have taken a good deal of courage to present a homicidal maniac with a message which would surely incense him, although the fact that Flad's wife and children were still captive must have been a powerful incentive. Theodore was predictably enraged, but he admired courage and sent the relieved Flad off to his family without harming him.

Theodore's main reaction to the message was defiance. If the British, he exclaimed, would not accept his friendship, let them come and fight, when he would certainly beat them. In spite of these bold words he must have realized in his more rational moments that his only real chance of defeating the British depended on the good will of his subjects, and this he had already forfeited. A year of fire and sword had turned the province into a desert. Gondar had been burnt to the ground, as had all the other towns and villages. Crops were few and scanty. Upwards of three thousand people had been killed with every refinement of torture, often for no apparent reason. The situation could not last, and finally, the angry inhabitants rose against him, cutting off stragglers from his army, and destroying their scant supplies of grain so that they should not fall into the hands of his hungry, oppressive soldiers. Many of the latter, appalled by his activities, deserted, but a hard core still stayed loyal.

Starvation was very close indeed, and Theodore in one of his more lucid periods faced the inevitable. He could no longer maintain himself or his dwindling army where he was. All that was left to him was Magdala, and on 10th October 1867 he burned Debra Tabor and set out for his last stronghold, a mad king with a dwindling army and no kingdom he could call his own except the ground within range of his guns. He was surrounded by enemies, but in spite of their increasing numbers and his own shrinking resources they did not attack. He was still Theodore, the warrior king, and his reputation was like a steel shield round him.

His army consisted of some seven thousand men, all that remained of his former host. About half were armed with reasonably modern small arms—mostly double-barrelled percussion guns of European manufacture—while the remainder mostly had old flint or matchlocks. Every man also had a sword, a spear, and a shield. Following Theodore too were thousands of useless mouths. They were mostly refugees from the areas he had devastated and they bore him no goodwill, but clung to him because where he went there might be a little food to beg or steal. In his train were his invaluable artisans, together with some hundreds of captives, mostly imprisoned for real or imagined political offences.

In this last phase, encompassed as he was by waiting enemies, much of his earlier military greatness returned to him. His main encumbrance was his train of artillery which included some pieces of enormous size. Without it he could have reached Magdala in a few easy marches but he would not abandon his last outward symbols of strength. His way lay across an almost trackless waste, traversed by mountains and cut with great ravines. Progress was painfully slow. Except for riding horses and mules he had no transport animals and the guns, carried on carts built by the versatile European workmen, had to be

H

dragged along by hand. The great mortar "Sebastopol", weighing nearly five tons, sometimes required eight hundred men on its drag ropes.

In the first six weeks after leaving Debra Tabor he averaged less than two miles a day, but he crawled on relentlessly. Great boulders had to be cleared away, causeways built across rivers, and roads engineered up and down sheer precipices. His over-worked soldiers, driven to desperation, took their chance at the hands of the angry rebels surrounding them and deserted by hundreds, and as many more died from a combination of exhaustion and starvation. And always his enemies hung on his flanks, killing stragglers, cutting off foraging parties, but never daring to close with his crew of ragged scarecrows. Nothing survived in his path, and people fled as he approached. He looted their corn and burned their villages mercilessly; if he caught any luckless villagers he burnt them too. The last grains of food were ferreted out, the last thin ox eaten by his hungry followers. Where he passed nothing lived.

All this time the King himself was in a state almost of exaltation and such was his prestige and influence that his men slaved for him, perhaps a little touched by his madness. One vast ravine held him up for a full three weeks but by incredible efforts he finally got across it, complete with guns. He soon found it necessary to release the artisans who had attempted to escape. There was nowhere for them to fly to in that wilderness and he needed their advice and assistance, especially in the matter of blasting. They responded nobly; it must be remembered that they were his private employees, and that in general he had treated them with generosity and consideration, although it is hard to say whether their efforts were due to loyalty or fear.

The terrible, relentless, crawl still took its toll by death or desertion, but it still went on—twenty great waggons and a few thousand desperate men, driven by one remarkable will and thinly sustained by an occasional capture of beef and grain—sometimes under the very noses of their enemies. These were increasing day by day. Wagshum Gobazi of Lasta and Menelik of Shoa alone had a combined army of vastly greater strength than Theodore's handful, but still they dared not strike.

The King came to the vast ravine of the Jedda, whose precipitous sides enclosed a vertical depth of three thousand two hundred feet. It was an apparently hopeless obstacle, but he tackled it resolutely. He himself selected the line of the path, and there followed a nightmare of blasting, digging, grading, and building. In four weeks of indescribable effort five miles of road were built, with very steep but very well planned gradients, and the guns lowered to the bed of the ravine. The wagons were edged down a few feet at a time with brakes on the wheels and hundreds of men preventing them from plunging to the bottom.

They then had to be got out on the other side and again the work started, a slow agony of ascent. But it was done—and done mainly by the relentless perseverance of one man. Theodore was never absent from the scene for a minute and he drove the workmen unremittingly, rewarding generously or cutting down ruthlessly according to merit, until the weaker part of his army was ground away, leaving a hard, desperate handful to finish the work. It took four more terrible weeks to get the wagons up, often a few inches at a time by the combined exertions of hundreds of sweating men, but it was done, and Theodore, his army, and his guns, were on the last plateau. Magdala was by then not far off; one more ravine remained at its foot; one more great effort would be required, and then the strange saga of these few thousand hopeless, naked, starving men under their mad King would be over. It is little known, and much of it was never chronicled, but it deserves its place among the great epics of Africa.

Theodore left the guns and the bulk of his army near the last ravine and rode on up the steep slope to Magdala with a handful of retainers. The prisoners in the fortress were understandably apprehensive, and Rassam sent off an obsequious message of welcome in the hopes of ensuring a good reception. As it turned out the King greeted them like old friends. On his approach bribery had lost much of its charms for their jailers, and although not actually ill-treated the prisoners had to submit to chains again. Theodore, however, at once ordered these to be removed.

He soon resumed his old intimacy with Rassam, and talked to

him for hours on a wide variety of subjects. Rassam was an intelligent, well educated, widely read man and it is likely that he had a calming influence on the king.

In spite of the astounding achievements of the march and the fact that he was securely back in his own fortress Theodore was for the most part very depressed. He knew of the approach of the British, still far to the north, and awaited their arrival with a strange mixture of anticipation and apprehension. He seemed to expect death, and his main fear was that he would not be given a decent burial. He told Rassam,

> One day you may see me dead, and, while you stand by my corpse you [will] curse me for having ill-treated you. You may say at the time, this wicked man ought not to be buried. But I trust to your generosity.

Prideaux and Blanc, being of Rassam's party, were also favoured and assured that come what may they would be safe. This may have comforted them a little, although they can hardly have put much reliance on his word, sincere though he may have been when he gave it. He had not drunk much on the march, but now that he was back in Magdala he began swilling arrack again and often fell into his old, wild, drunken rages.

On 2nd April the last piece of his ordnance remaining in the valley, the great mortar, was finally brought up to Islamgi, the plateau just below the main fortress, and Theodore with great geniality invited all his European prisoners to come and watch the operation. He himself supervised it, and presently the great mass of brass in its crude, solid cart, was brought safely to the top. As soon as it was up he ordered a salute to be fired from all guns, after which he lost interest and retired to his tent and his arrack.

A few days later he ordered all his political prisoners, some five hundred and seventy of them, to be brought to Islamgi. After much thought he released a number of the more important chiefs and the women and children and then returned to drinking, leaving the remainder of his captives exposed on the hillside without food, water, or shelter.

Theodore was very soon in a stupor and all might have been

well had he not been roused by the wailing of the prisoners crying for water. This put him into one of his mad, irrational rages and he at once ordered that they should all be put to death. He himself set an example by cutting down several with his sword and shooting two more with his pistol, after which his soldiers set to work. Nearly two hundred were flung down the cliff, some still in chains, some with their hands and feet cut off, after which the soldiers amused themselves by firing their muskets at any which still showed signs of life.

The King's rage then evaporated as quickly as it had risen. He called a halt to the slaughter and sent the terrified survivors back to their prison in Magdala. Then he returned to his tent and spent the rest of the night in remorseful prayer, constantly calling on God to believe that it was drink which had caused him to do it. Below, far down the hillside, a few of the victims still showed signs of life, moving a little and calling for water, but by dawn all was quiet.

The next morning Theodore, apparently perfectly normal again, began to think about putting his fortress in a state of defence. He had several of his heaviest guns and mortars moved to Fala where he sited them to cover the approaches from the north, but left the remainder on Islamgi. While this was being done he asked Waldemeier what he thought he ought to do, and was strongly advised to sue for peace. This angered him. He fired a pistol at Waldemeier, and when it failed to go off he flung a spear at him which missed, upon which the missionary, inferring that his advice was not altogether welcome, withdrew hastily.

As soon as his artillery was in position Theodore stationed himself on the highest point of the fortress and thereafter spent much of his time with an excellent glass watching for the British. He was a soldier, and had been a good one, and he had heard so much of the disciplined armies of Europe that he longed above all things to see one in action, even though it should be against him. At times he believed defeat and death to be near; at others he was convinced that the British were coming as friends to help him destroy his enemies and place him firmly back on his throne so that he might yet lead his great crusade against the Moslem

117

oppressors of his people. All the while the rebel chiefs and the wild Gallas were gathering expectantly, only waiting for the moment when the British should blast him out of his great fortress.

His army should not be underestimated. The weaker elements had died or deserted and those remaining were the hard core, the men who had built the road through the wilderness and hauled the guns along it. Now they were firmly ensconced in a near impregnable fortress, well supplied with guns and ammunition, and if they chose to fight it was certain that the advancing British would suffer many casualties—possible even, that they might sustain a crushing defeat. They had to take the fortress by a swift *coup-de-main* or starve, and a *coup-de-main*, if it failed, might mean disaster; a slow retreat through the mountains, short of food and ammunition and encumbered with hundreds of casualties. The pickings would be too good to miss, and every chief along the route would come hurrying down for his share. On the way south all that had been taken from the British had been thousands of dollars. On the way north it might be thousands of even more desirable articles—modern firearms.

* * *

Far to the north Napier and his troops were making steady progress. They were vastly better equipped than Theodore and did not have enormous guns to move but their march was arduous and both mules and men were becoming exhausted by the eternal rock scrambling—now slipping and sliding down a steep slope at imminent risk of a broken leg—now crawling up some almost sheer rock face.

The march to Dildi was the worst the troops had experienced. Conditions were appalling, and to make things worse there were indications that the locals had been systematically destroying the path. Captain Hayward, who marched over it a few days later with the 45th Regiment (hastening forward to catch the main body), said that they,

Ascended by a bad and stony path following the right bank of the stream which runs through a fairly open but steep valley for about four and a half miles, the sides of the valley being covered in bush. The road, having reached the head of the valley about fifteen hundred feet above our starting point, makes a sudden drop almost perpendicularly by a zig-zag path cut in the bank of a ravine for about eight hundred feet and then, following the left bank of a deep, rugged watercourse, winds along the side of a precipitous mountain—or rather a succession of mountains until it attains the top of a spur some twelve or thirteen thousand feet above the level of the sea. Thence by a succession of steep rises and falls it leads to the camp of Dildie. . . . It was the hardest day's march we have had, the country being excessively hilly and trying.

It was here that the 33rd blotted its copy-book. Although a Yorkshire regiment, it had a high proportion of Irishmen in its ranks—so many indeed that Stanley almost always referred to it as "the Irish Regiment". This was not an unusual state of affairs in the British Army. Ireland in the nineteenth century was truly a "distressful country" due mainly to a combination of absentee landlords, rapacious agents, a backward agriculture, and a teeming, ignorant peasantry. There was a steady exodus of young men from the country.

Many went west to America, but a great number made their way to England, desperately seeking work, and of these a good many inevitably fell into the hands of the recruiting sergeants. Free-born Englishmen might sneer at peacetime soldiering and fight shy of enlisting, but the Irish had no such inhibitions. To a ragged young man brought up in a smoky sod cabin on a diet of potatoes and butter-milk, the army offered standards he had never dreamed of. Beef, bread, beer, a dry bed under a sound roof, smart clothes, even a few coppers in his pocket.

These men were in a sense true mercenaries. Often in their own minds they owed no allegiance to the Queen and hated her government, but they made excellent soldiers, and the British Army would have been in sorry state without them.

The soldiers of the 33rd were big, mature men—rough, foul-mouthed, and heavy drinkers, but they were steady and imposing on parade and they had worked like slaves at Zula and on the

119

route south. The terrible pull up to Dildi was the last straw; the trouble started with much straggling and a good deal of audible (and probably unprintable) comment on the expedition as a whole, and both got rapidly worse. Dozens of men lay down and refused to move. Staff officers were jeered at, their own officers for the moment ignored. Only a handful marched into camp with the colours; the remainder straggled in throughout the night.

The episode was in many ways a minor one. An officer of the regiment said later that discipline had been deteriorating slowly for some time, and attributed it by implication to a lack of firmness on the part of Dunn—which may or may not be fair. It is certain that his predecessor had been much more of a martinet, but it seems at least possible that a man of Dunn's record and personality might have averted the incident. It is certain that after a night's rest the regiment was as steady as it ever had been.

General Napier was not pleased. He was a pleasant, courteous man but he could be firm and he decided to be in this case. Next morning he had the regiment paraded and addressed them forcibly. What he said hurt. They were a disgrace to the expedition and certainly not fit to lead the advance; they would drop back, and the 4th Kings Own would be brought forward in their place. The 33rd winced, for the two regiments had been together in Poona where there had been great rivalry between them, both in work and play, and they could imagine the comments which would be made. The Commander-in-Chief was as good as his word; the 4th were sent for and by a double forced march reached the head of the column in two days, during which time the remainder halted at Dildi.

The march then continued, the brigades moving a day apart. They climbed and kept climbing, often through clinging mist and occasional torrential rain which soon churned the ground into liquid mud. Life was dull and hard, but from time to time it was at least enlivened by rumours. One of the most persistent was that M. Munzinger had been captured by one of the King's patrols; another was that Theodore was advancing with the intention of disputing the crossing of the deep, precipitous Takazze Ravine which lay some miles further south.

Both, as it turned out, proved false, but the second caused Napier some concern. He accelerated the rate of march and soon the leading brigade were scrambling down the steep descent of the Takazze to the river. The south bank rose precipitously for some four thousand feet and the sappers and pioneers at once set to work to make a practicable track up it. The tired foot soldiers looked at the prospect and groaned, but went on. Behind them a well-mounted newspaper correspondent watched with sympathetic admiration as the "iron souls of the 4th" (as he described them) began the long, slow torment.

The whole face of the hillside was soon covered with gasping soldiers and exhausted animals, creeping upwards as best they could without order or cohesion. The last few yards of the hill were precipitous and the track rose in a series of wide zig-zag scarps, so that a tired staff officer leading an even more tired charger found to his exasperation that people within easy hailing distance above him were a good half mile ahead of him in terms of actual marching. It took a whole day to get the leading brigade up, but by nightfall the southern edge was firmly held and the chances of an Abyssinian attack much reduced.

There was no longer any comfort, other than a blanket and the twentieth share of a small bell-tent on a bare rocky hillside. Even the rum had run out and although a few prudent officers might still have a bottle or two concealed, the bulk of the column made do with milkless, sugarless, tea. Even the sick suffered. They could not be left and were carried on in *doolis*, their bearers slipping and stumbling on the rocky, muddy surface.

Napier's ADC chose this moment to develop raging toothache and suffered agonies, but wrapped his head in a scarf against the wind and kept going. Fortunately he had hoarded some rum which helped to deaden the pain. Dental officers did not exist in those days, and none of the British medical officers had any dental tools, but presently a diligent search produced from the kit of the Indian doctor of a native regiment, an old-fashioned key extractor. The staff surgeon at once set to work with this and succeeded in extracting a rotten back tooth. No anaesthetic was used—the limited chloroform was reserved for possible sterner uses further south—so that the operation was a painful

121

one, but it removed the cause of the trouble and enabled a somewhat shaken young man to keep going. He had no intention of missing the "show" after having come so far to see it.

Water, although not scarce, was frequently inaccessible. The unfortunate animals sometimes had to be led for hundreds of feet down precipitous paths, and any enthusiast who wished to bathe had to do the same. A few did, but the bulk preferred to go dirty.

Headquarters and the leading brigade arrived at Santara on 28th March and there Sir Robert halted for a few days to allow the troops behind him to close up. While there he received a visit from the envoy of Wagshum Gobazi (the ruler of Lasta), who was a rebel against Theodore and a rival of the Prince of Tigré. Gobazi was an ambitious man but a very cautious one—some said a coward—and preferred not to deal with the British direct, presumably to allow himself some sort of escape if by any chance the King won.

The envoy arrived unexpectedly with a strong body of cavalry which caused the pickets to turn out in some haste, and the Abyssinian horsemen made a considerable impression on the British by galloping down an almost precipitous slope in good order. The envoy was entertained, made a number of vague promises of help followed by the usual request on behalf of his master for armed assistance against his rivals, and departed.

CHAPTER 9
The Final Advance

SANTARA was situated on the northern edge of the Dalenta Plateau, not more than seven or eight marches from Magdala, and Napier decided to halt there and make dispositions for his final advance. The delay was to some extent forced on him by a shortage of supplies sufficiently serious to make him at least consider the necessity for a further cut in the already austere daily ration.

There were three reasons for this shortage; in the first place Theodore's agents had been busy spreading the news that actually the British were coming as friends in order to restore him to his throne, a prospect very alarming to the local inhabitants; next was the simple fact that local supplies just did not exist in the quantities needed, for the area had been well within range of the King's foraging parties during his march and had thus been left a desert; third, and by far the most annoying, was that petty local chiefs along the route were interfering with local transport. They had begun levying a tax, or what might better be called a blackmail, on the contract carriers, and this simple and lucrative practice had soon reached the stage where the system was in danger of collapsing completely.

The problem was political, and soon Merewether's officers were busy visiting local chiefs explaining, cajoling, and where necessary, threatening. This quickly had its effect and supplies again began to come in. It was indeed noticeable that even the areas recently devastated by Theodore's army were apparently able to produce grain in considerable quantities. Much of it had been concealed in large, narrow-mouthed pits, and it is said that the method adopted by Theodore's soldiers to discover such stores, was to extend across any likely looking open space and dance forward in line hoping that the stamping rhythm would reveal the hollow places underground. It is clear from the quantities eventually brought in to the Commissariat that the method cannot have been highly successful.

Sir Charles Staveley marched in with the second brigade on the 30th March. The brigade was preceded by the 33rd Regiment which marched in gaily to the appropriate, if slightly insubordinate, strains of *Here we are again* which its band was thumping out with great gusto.

When the whole force had assembled the *ad hoc* third brigade was broken up and its units reallocated to the other two brigades which formed the 1st Division under Staveley. Some troops were still well behind and coming up by forced marches, but as soon as the supply situation eased the General decided that it would be as well to continue southwards. Austerity was now the order of the day, and for everyone. All ranks from Napier downwards ate the same food; tough beef, chupattis, and a few compressed vegetables, with a little tea. Fortunately the countryside yielded large quantities of excellent honey, a useful substitute for sugar.

Even game for the pot had become scarce, since few officers had bothered to bring guns so far, not so much because of their weight as because of the impossibility of obtaining cartridges. The intelligence department had also always been eager to buy guns at good prices as presents for deserving chiefs and headmen along the way, so that a number of the more commercially minded owners of sporting weapons had taken the opportunity of relieving themselves of some unwelcome weight and making a substantial profit in the bargain.

The troops were showing signs of exhaustion but were generally in good shape and keen to get on now that their goal was so close. The fittest and most cheerful members of the force were undoubtedly the Naval Brigade. They were also very efficient, particularly as muleteers. Few of them knew anything about animal transport but care and common sense seemed an excellent substitute for experience. The sailors' general, proverbial handiness also made it natural for them to adjust saddles and lash loads neatly and securely so that their beasts were amongst the best cared for in the force.

Jack ashore was always popular with the army, and these were no exception. Rather strangely they had become particularly friendly with the Punjab pioneer battalion of Musby Sikhs and although they had no common language they seemed to manage very well. In the evenings one of the sights of the camp was the sailors—still full of life after weeks of arduous marching—dancing energetically to the cheerful music of the pioneer's band.

The weather was variable. The days were pleasant, temperatures often being in the seventies, but at night time it was not unusual for water bottles to freeze solid, even in a laced tent full of men. It was as well that tents and warm clothing had been carried, cumbersome though they were, for without them the sick rate would probably have been high. Fuel was short which added to the discomfort. The locals produced enough for basic cooking but not for the sort of roaring fires which night temperatures demanded. Some genius found large deposits of rock which had all the outward appearance of coal and was much downcast after a great deal of fruitless experiment, to find that it would not burn.

Now that Napier was nearing Magdala his line of approach gave him some cause for thought. There were still two large ravines, both easily defensible, between his force and the objective and he considered making a wide circuit east so as to cross them as close to their heads as possible. M. Munzinger, who had made a careful reconnaissance of the country in that direction, reported however that the ground was extremely broken and difficult and did not recommend the attempt. Napier then decided to take the direct route, which had the advantage that it would quickly bring him onto the excellent track engineered by Theodore only a few weeks before. The only disadvantage of using the route was that it was such an obvious line of approach that Theodore might be tempted to try to hold one of the difficult ravine crossings on it; but the risk was slight and well worth taking in view of the time and work which was likely to be saved by using the King's own road.

Extensive precautions were taken against ambush. Unidentified horsemen, presumed to be Abyssinian scouts, were seen from time to time, and as it was known that Theodore particularly favoured night attacks, pickets and vedettes were made very strong.

This heightened air of expectancy led to an incident which might have had unfortunate results. A visit by Mashesha, uncle and envoy of Wagshum Gobazi, to Napier's headquarters with 1st Brigade, was concluded satisfactorily and the chief and his followers (about two hundred horsemen) were escorted beyond the pickets on their way home. Unfortunately their route back lay close to the outpost line of the 2nd Brigade a mile or two in rear, and their appearance caused some apprehension. The nearest post, an NCO and three men of the 3rd Cavalry, at once turned out, and having had no notice of any friendly locals in the area warned the horsemen off. The Abyssinians, with their love of display, took no notice but jeered, waved their swords and spears, and made a show of charging. At this, the outpost, understandably convinced that here at last was the enemy, fired a quick volley from their carbines and at once charged sword in hand. The Abyssinians fled, hotly pursued by the angry cavalrymen who actually ran two of them through with swords. By this time all the outposts were alerted, the 2nd Brigade had turned out on its alarm posts, and a troop of cavalry had taken up the pursuit before the error was discovered and the troops called off. Two Abyssinians were killed and one wounded in this unfortunate affair, and the invaluable M. Munzinger was at once sent off post-haste to the chief concerned to offer condolences, apologies, explanations, and compensation. All these were readily accepted and the affair soon forgotten. Not the least notable aspect of it is the unhesitating gallantry with which the unknown Indian NCO led his little party out against odds of fifty to one.

On 3rd April Napier sent off a final letter to Theodore demanding the release of the prisoners, and next day the advance continued. The crossing of the Jedda Ravine was accompanied more quickly than had been expected, thanks to the previous work put in by the King's army. The track up was very steep and the march a tiring one but by the afternoon the force were all over the obstacle. The area on the other side was not prepossessing:

> A bare plain, not a stick of food for man or beast within sight—nothing but the bare, undulating plain, old ploughed ground, and the remains of fields or what were once fields; a few piles of stones to show where a village had been razed to the ground; very cold; no tents up; getting dusk and a dropping rain; soft ploughed land on which we are encamped; no firewood, not a tree in the countryside apparently; nothing but a few pools of water which we gladly go to, to give our horses a drink after their exertions. Theodore has left his mark here; his destroying army is like a flight of locusts . . . he has eaten up the land; and not content with that, he has burnt and destroyed the villages. There is hardly one stone left standing on another, and the people have all fled.

Here the force again halted, partly to close up and partly to seek supplies. The locals were understandably dubious about the good faith of the British, but Captain Speedy rode indefatigably round the surrounding countryside trying to dispel the rumour that they had come as allies to Theodore, and his efforts quickly proved effective. In spite of the desolation all round, grain was soon coming into the market in surprising quantities.

Sir Robert Napier rode forward from there, and three or four miles further south reached the Beshilo Ravine, from the edge of which Magdala was clearly visible. It was a great moment, and everyone surveyed the huge rock mass eagerly with their glasses, but there was nothing to be seen except a little smoke.

Off to the north-east could also be seen the towering pillar of Amba Geshen, another natural rock fortress, on the summit of which huts and trees could be identified. Until the fifteenth century it had been the traditional place of detention for the

127

brothers of the ruling king; they were never allowed their freedom in case they should plot against him.

* * *

On 9th April the headquarters wing of the 45th Regiment arrived in camp, having marched up from the coast with only one halt. They had been warned rather late for the expedition and had remained in their barracks at Poona for some time, doubtful if they would be required at all, until firm orders for their move were received on 10th January. Some word of the transport problems in Abyssinia had obviously filtered back to India, for Captain Hayward wrote in his diary,

> Our ascent from the lowland to Senafé will be after the manner of a balloon with the wretched baggage animals we shall get; the more we ascend the more we shall have to throw away!

He therefore sensibly had a final thin-out of his kit before going down to parade his company, who had been celebrating in the manner traditional to British soldiers but who were nevertheless on the whole "fairly sober", only one or two being "rather overcome".

The 45th arrived at Zula on 2nd February and there the battalion split. The right or headquarters wing was warned to be ready to move forward as an escort for a large convoy of dollars, while the left wing learnt to its dismay that it was destined for garrison duties—at least until the 26th Cameronians should arrive. There was a fairly long and boring delay at Zula, spent for the most part at drill, road-making, or on shooting parties. During this period the battalion was highly amused by their assistant surgeon, Wood, who having been detailed for an inquest on an Indian, solemnly completed all the written work first, including a verdict of "found dead", and then went to inspect the body—only to find it alive and recovering from a monumental drunk.

Eventually baggage animals and dollars were assembled and on 9th March the half-battalion set off. The 45th had always enjoyed a certain reputation for marching; over fifty years before, in the Peninsula, Lieutenant Grattan of the 88th, after extolling the marching powers of his own wild Irishmen from the bogs of Connaught, had gone on to describe,

> That first rate battle Regiment, the 45th, a parcel of Nottingham weavers whose sedentary habits would lead you to suppose that they could not be prime marchers; but the contrary was the fact, and they marched to the full as well as my own corps. . . .

The 45th had not lost their old endurance, and were able to march on solidly, mile after mile, day after day, in their anxiety not to miss anything that was going to happen to the south. The duties of the baggage guard were particularly arduous—Captain Hayward's diary from 19th March contains the single terse comment, "Indians say that Europeans won't work. Let them come to Abyssinia and see." This routine continued until 1st April when the battalion, although in excellent shape, was compelled to halt for three days because of the exhausted state of the baggage animals. Then they went on, and after a gruelling last lap, caught up with the main body on 8th April. The final climb to the Dalenta Plateau was particularly arduous for rain had made the steep track slippery and the animals suffered accordingly. At one stage the elephants caused a major holdup. The leading beast, heavily loaded, began to slide backwards and there was a wild scramble of soldiers and mules to get out of the way of this juggernaut. The elephant, a female, managed to stop her undignified descent after fifty yards but her companions wisely refused to risk the same fate and remained stubbornly where they were until the patch had dried out. After the 8th April the situation improved and the 45th, who until then had carried their own bedding, were allotted mules for the purpose, a great relief to the heavily laden soldiers. General Napier, referring to their march in his despatch of 1st June wrote,

> The headquarters and six companies making most strenuous efforts to reach the front, arrived at Dalenta in time to share in the operations against Magdala after having marched 300 miles in 24 days, accomplishing the last 70 miles

across the Wandach Pass, 10,500 feet high and the Taccassi and Jedda Ravines in four days, a rate of marching in such a country hardly to be surpassed.

The next day, the force moved to the northern edge of the Beshilo Ravine, whence Magdala was clearly visible. Across the ravine a side valley, down which ran a stream, led up to a broken tableland, and immediately beyond it stood two features, Selassi on the left and Fala on the right, joined by a saddle. Magdala was immediately behind Selassi and its summit could be seen just above it.

The force camped on the plateau while the sappers, the Punjab Pioneers, and a wing of the Baluchis went on down the King's road to start work in preparation for the descent of the main body to the river. While this was being done envoys were sent off to the Galla people requesting their help in cutting off Theodore's retreat should he decide to withdraw rather than face the British. Napier, true to his policy of avoiding involvement in the internal affairs of the country, took this step with some hesitation. It was forced on him by the enormous extent of the Fala-Selassi-Magdala massif, far too large to invest fully with the troops he had at his disposal.

His principal emissary was a Moslem Indian from Hyderabad, one Meer Akbir Ali attached to the intelligence department; he had been selected chiefly because the local Gallas also happened to be Moslems and it was hoped that the common religion would give him a strong claim on their services. In this he was successful. At first the Gallas were extremely distrustful of the goodwill of the British and obviously feared that they would eventually be left to the mercies of Theodore, of whom they were clearly terrified. Eventually however, all was settled and they agreed to help hem in the king should he try to bolt southwards.

The stay at the Beshilo camp was marked by heavy rain, thunder and hail, so that the force was glad of its tents. Orders had been given that they were not to be carried any further; from then onwards everyone was to sleep in the open, and it was not a prospect which anyone relished.

By day there was no apparent activity on the great rock bastion opposite them, but by night the summit of Magdala glowed red with hundreds of fires, and it was possible with a good glass to see dark wild figures moving round them. Here at last was the enemy, and if only the Gallas played their part the campaign should soon be over; Theodore would either have to negotiate, which would be something of an anticlimax, or fight, which was what most of the force were hoping for. Nevertheless it occurred to some of the more experienced officers that if the King's men resisted stoutly Magdala might be a tough nut to crack. The force was not well-equipped with heavy guns, nor was there much siege material available. The sappers did what they could by improvising scaling ladders from dooli poles and making up powder charges for blowing in gates, but it seemed little enough against the vast natural strength of the fortress facing them.

While on the Dalenta Plateau Napier made as detailed a reconnaissance of his objective as was possible in the circumstances. Much of it was done by means of a good glass from the edge of the ravine, but he also rode down the King's road, as far as the Beshilo river which was a narrow, muddy stream, not more than three feet deep and thus easily fordable.

On the south side of the stream the road ran up the bottom of the deep valley of the Warki-Waha and Napier did not like the look of it. It was bounded on both sides by steep rocky banks, and was thus likely to prove a death trap unless those banks could be held firmly by infantry pickets. Shortage of men however made this impossible. The point where the road rose out of the ravine was also within long artillery range of Fala, whence a plunging fire might be brought to bear on it, although the probable poor quality of Theodore's gunners did not make this such a serious threat as it might have been against better-trained opponents.

It was very clear to the Commander-in-Chief that he was too far back to make any detailed plans against Magdala, so he decided that he would make a reconnaissance in force across the river, establish himself in some strength on the tableland below Fala, and complete his detailed planning when he had had more opportunities of a closer inspection of the ground.

In view of the dangerous appearance of the King's road he

decided to leave the ravine severely alone initially and move further to his right up the long Gumbaji-Afficho spur, at the top of which he reckoned on finding a secure camp-site on the Arogi Plateau. It was possible that it would be within range of Theodore's artillery but he was confident that his own well-handled guns, mortars and rockets would have no difficulty in subduing the Abyssinian fire.

On 9th April an operation order was issued for a move next morning, the general intention being that the 1st Brigade would lead the way up the Gumbaji-Afficho spur accompanied by Phayre, who was then to carry out a detailed reconnaissance further forward. Four companies of sappers were to follow the Brigade and improve the track sufficiently for the mules and elephants to negotiate it. Napier, from his distant reconnaissance had reckoned, rightly, that the path, although very steep, could be made passable. The 2nd Brigade was to move to the bed of the Beshilo with the cavalry and there await such further orders as the results of Phayre's probing might dictate. All being well it was hoped that by nightfall the bulk of the force would be firmly established in the area of Arogi.

The main administrative problem was likely to be the provision of water. A small stream ran down the ravine but it was dangerous and difficult of access, so that the most likely secure source of water was the Beshilo. As part of his arrangements the General therefore organized proper water parties of transport mules under command of a Commissariat officer. Strict orders were given regarding water discipline and all ranks were ordered to fill their water bottles while fording the Beshilo.

CHAPTER 10
Battle At Arogi

T HE advance started at daybreak on 10th April 1868. It was Good Friday, perhaps the strangest that any member of the expedition would ever see. The march was exhausting. The rocky road down to the river, dropping three thousand five hundred feet in five miles, was treacherous for the heavily laden infantry and the pace was slow. There was a good deal of crowding and confusion at the river itself, for the troops had been ordered to remove their boots and socks before fording it, and although this was a sensible—perhaps essential—precaution for health reasons it seemed dangerous in such close proximity to a hostile army; it also wasted a good deal of time.

Most of the men had emptied their water bottles on the scramble down in anticipation of being able to refill them at the river, but when they reached it they found the water so churned up and muddy at the ford that many of them refused to touch it, and went on with empty canteens.

Eventually the long, steep pull up the Gumbaji spur began, led by the Punjab Pioneers, and it was at this stage that things started to go slightly wrong. Colonel Phayre, riding in advance with the divisional commander (who although almost crippled with rheumatism had resolutely refused to miss the chance of action) decided to alter the plan. This was unusual, but possibly justified in the light of a closer survey of the ground. Certainly General Staveley appears to have made no comment when a message to that effect was passed back through him to the

Commander-in-Chief. The modification proposed by Phayre was that as the path was very steep and difficult he would take the sappers on with him and establish them in a strong position where the King's road debouched onto the plateau. The guns and baggage could then, he reckoned, safely follow the easier route up.

On receipt of this message Napier, who had implicit trust in Phayre, made no demur but at once despatched the mountain guns, the Naval Brigade, and the baggage of the 1st Brigade up the road. He then rode off with his staff along the steep Gumbaji track. About four miles up it, he passed the 4th Kings Own fallen out on the side of the path, exhausted and calling for water. Further on the Baluchis were still steadily climbing the appalling track, while immediately ahead of them the Punjab Pioneers were just beginning to debouch onto the level plain of Arogi.

The Commander-in-Chief reached the plateau at about the same time as the leading elements of the Pioneers, and there he found Staveley and Phayre, together with the sapper companies. No record exists of the discussion which must then have taken place, but it is clear that something had gone wrong. The most likely cause seems to be that Napier, miscalculating the length of time needed for heavily laden foot soldiers to reach Arogi, had sent the guns and baggage off too soon up the relatively easy ascent of the King's road. Phayre was a capable and experienced soldier and it is inconceivable that he would have neglected to hold the ravine entrance when he himself had suggested the change of plan which made it necessary. Nor is it in the least likely that Staveley would have allowed the omission.

Napier acted quickly. His first action was to send the pioneers off to the mouth of the ravine, twelve hundred yards away and seven hundred feet below him, across a wilderness of rock, sand, and scrub. At the same time an ADC was sent back to bring up the 4th at all speed; a situation was likely to arise when Napier would require infantry, British infantry at that, and it might arise very quickly.

The ADC, realizing the possible seriousness of the situation, rode off at a gallop. A train of mules, laden with water or ammunition, was scrambling up the narrow path and there was hardly room for him to pass, but he set his teeth, took the inside, and hoped for the best. At the narrowest part he felt his boot strike violently against a mule's load, and heard the wail of the muleteer as his unfortunate beast fell forty feet onto the rocks below. Then he was clear at last, and soon reached the still recumbent 4th. The battalion got wearily to its feet at his summons and started off up the track. The men looked beaten but discipline told—besides there was a certain feeling of urgency inspired by a galloping staff officer—a faint hope that something more congenial than rock climbing might be in the wind.

Young Scott, the ADC concerned, at once turned his horse and hurried back to his General, who was still where he had been left, watching the scene before him. High up on Fala they could see seven guns with Abyssinians busy about them, an ominous promise of things to come, but there was nothing to do now but to wait and see what happened. For the moment the initiative was with the King.

Far off to the left the pioneers reached the mouth of the ravine just as the Naval Brigade emerged from it. Captain Fellowes, seeing the guns and their busy crews high above him, drew his own conclusions and swung right towards Arogi. Behind him came the mountain battery, and it too swung right up the hill, but only for a couple of hundred yards. Colonel Millward's orders had been to find a suitable camp-site above the head of the gorge and this he set about doing. He too had seen the guns above him but they did not worry him unduly. Guns were his business and he probably reckoned that he was well out of range of anything except random shot.

General Napier still sat composedly on his charger, watching the guns on Fala. He realized that he had been caught off balance; he was too far forward and had the wrong troops in front, but he had had enough experience of savage enemies to know that even a short withdrawal would seem to have been caused by the threat of Theodore's artillery, and would raise the morale of the Abyssinians accordingly. Napier therefore determined to stay where he was. Soon he heard the scrape of boots on rock and the clatter of accoutrements, and looking round saw that the 4th Regiment had arrived and were flopping down groaning on the path behind him. Tired though they were he was relieved to have them, for he had seen enough of the recuperative powers of British soldiers in the desperate days of the Mutiny to know that the prospect of action would have a powerful effect on them. He turned again to the guns above him and raised his glass to examine them. As he did so a puff of grey smoke rolled from one of them and a heavy roundshot came howling down to plump into the ground close behind him. It was at last clear that Theodore was going to fight.

As Napier had anticipated, the effect on the 4th was miraculous; hardly had the wind carried the billowing smoke away before every man was on his feet, scrambling into his equipment and cheering wildly. Fatigue was forgotten. This was what they had marched four hundred miles for. What were dry tongues and sore feet with a battle in prospect?

The slow cannonade continued. The General, who had been under worse fire in his day, never stirred, but some of the younger members of his staff had to stiffen themselves in their saddles so as not to duck instinctively each time a ball came whirring down. Some were chain-shot, in which the two halves of a ball were linked by a length of chain. They were primarily intended for use in naval battles to cut rigging, and it is not clear why Theodore's gunners were using them, but they made a particularly ominous noise on their way down.

Up on the plateau Theodore had opened the engagement with some hesitation and under a serious, although understandable, misapprehension. Almost all he could see were long columns of mules issuing steadily from the mouth of the defile and he leapt to the conclusion, not wholly wrongly, that the British for some reason had their baggage in the lead. This was the chance to strike an easy blow, to stiffen the morale of his army, and to give them an opportunity for the plundering they loved. His plan was quickly made; he would paralyze the British with his irresistible artillery and send his army swarming down under cover of the cannonade. Theodore sent back a message for his troops to be brought up, and gave the order for his guns to open fire. The guns had been loaded and laid by his European artisans (who were unlikely to have been anxious to do any damage to the approaching British). In any case the technical problems involved would have been considerable, even for highly skilled gunners, since a variety of calibres and lengths had to be laid at a target at almost extreme range and far below them.

The artisans appear to have tackled the problem by loading the guns as heavily as they dared, and letting someone else fire them. One of the first pieces discharged, a heavy fifty-six pounder named *Theodorus* after its owner, burst at the first round and killed or crippled a number of gunners. This made the King furious for the moment but his anger soon dissolved in the excitement of battle. Technical difficulties were lost on him; his guns were booming away and he was convinced that nothing could stand against them.

Old Fitaurari Gabri, his favourite General, was now up with him, resplendent in an embroidered scarlet cloak and shirt, having left his troops squatting a few yards back from the edge of the Fala saddle. Theodore explained the situation briefly, and as his troops roared their approval of his plan he waved them forward against the British.

*   *   *

Far below on the plateau the watching soldiers saw the sudden activity along the crest above them as a great horde of men— some six or seven thousand of them—swarmed suddenly over the edge of the saddle and came dropping from rock to rock down the steep hillside, the sun glinting on their swords and spears. There was no organized body of cavalry with them, but some five hundred of their chiefs and principal men were riding either mules or sure-footed Galla ponies, which seemed to nego- tiate the almost precipitous drop with as much ease as the foot- men. At the bottom of the slope the swarm stopped for a moment to extend its front and then came on again at a steady jog-trot, a great loose swathe of fighting men, six or seven deep and three quarters of a mile wide.

A brief order went back from Napier, and the 4th Regiment moved on past the Staff and down into the shallow depression

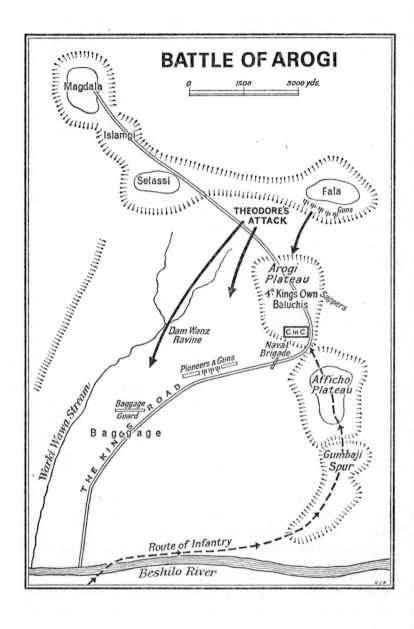

BATTLE OF AROGI

0   1500   3000 yds.

Magdala

Islamgi

Selassi

Fala

Guns

THEODORE'S
ATTACK

*Arogi
Plateau*

4th Kings Own
Baluchis

Sappers

C. in C.

Dam Wanz
Ravine

Naval
Brigade

*Afficho
Plateau*

Pioneers & Guns

THE KING'S ROAD

Baggage
Guard

B a g g a g e

*Gumbaji
Spur*

Warki Wawa Stream

Route of Infantry

Beshilo River

H.J.R

in front of them. As they advanced up the gentle slope on the other side they extended into skirmishing order and halted on the crest. There were not many of them; two companies had been detached as brigade baggage guard, and inevitably there were a few sick and stragglers, so that the main body probably did not number more than three hundred rifles.

The companies of sappers formed at an angle to them, so as to cover their right flank, while the Baluchis closed up in support.

* * *

Far off to the left Colonel Millward abandoned his search for a camp-site somewhat abruptly as the Abyssinians erupted over the crest. Instead he had the guns taken off the mules and formed in line on a small hillock, after which there was nothing to do except wait until the enemy came within effective range. The Punjab Pioneers, seeing the apparently defenceless state of the battery, formed hastily on either flank, then they too waited expectantly.

The sailors came into action first. As the Naval Brigade reached the edge of the Arogi Plateau they halted, set up their tubes and sent a stream of rockets hissing and spluttering off towards the charging line. The rocket was not, at best, a particularly accurate weapon, and dozens of them burst harmlessly far away from their target. Here and there however, gaps appeared momentarily in the line as well (or luckily) placed missiles burst over it, but the Abyssinians still came on with great determination, apparently undeterred by the strange, fiery projectiles. As they got closer they split into two sections, one of which came on towards the Kings Own while the other veered off down the valley towards the little line of silent guns.

* * *

On the right, the thin khaki skirmishing line of the Kings Own waited expectantly. Here and there a man moved his feet impatiently or fumbled at his cartridge box, but for the most part they remained still, leaning quietly on their untried Sniders and watching Theodore's advancing army. Old Gabri, conspicuous in scarlet, rode in the centre of the line and many of the 4th, believing him to be Theodore, had marked him down in their minds as their first target.

In the centre, near the colours, Colonel Cameron also watched intently, gauging the range and speed of movement of the enemy. He was an experienced officer who knew his business and he wanted the first blast of musketry to be a devastating one, so that although the Snider was effective at five hundred yards he waited resolutely. When the approaching line was some two hundred and fifty yards away he judged the time ripe. He took a firmer grip of his reins, cast a final glance left and right along the line of intent, bearded faces, then in a clear, unhurried voice gave the order to fire.

Three hundred blue barrels came up together, and three hundred hammers clicked back to full cock. The first burst of fire ran down the line with a noise like a great tearing of canvas and a wide gap appeared abruptly in the centre of the Abyssinian line as the storm of fire hit it.

Old Gabri and hundreds more went down at the first discharge and the whole line reeled and hesitated, but then came on gallantly. Theodore's fighting men, used only to muzzle-loaders, apparently anticipated a decent interval while the slow ritual of powder and ball, rod and cap was obeyed, but it was not granted them.

The British were firing independently and by the time the more deliberate shots had fired their first rounds the quicker men were ready with their second. The fire was therefore continuous; six or eight rounds a minute were quite possible with the Snider, so that the line was probably producing thirty or forty well aimed shots each second. Not a lot, to be sure, by modern standards, but remarkable then. With the possible exception of some of the foreign observers, no one present had previously seen breech-loaders in action, and to men accustomed to volleys the fire was frightening in its intensity. Fortunately too, a stiff breeze took the smoke away so that the target was never obscured for a moment.

Theodore's unfortunate warriors went down by hundreds until

presently the line, scourged beyond endurance, wavered, stopped, and fled. One group of fifty or sixty came relatively unscathed to within a hundred yards of the British line before turning to flee; then the fire swept through it, and men and mounts went down in kicking heaps.

As the Abyssinians went back the Kings Own began a steady advance, firing more slowly as suitable targets offered themselves. After their first precipitate retreat Theodore's men showed no further sign of panic but withdrew quietly, turning from time to time to discharge their smoothbore guns at their tormentors. A few of the bravest actually attempted to stand, and taking cover behind rocks opened a sharp fire on the advancing line. For the first time in the battle the Abyssinian musketry could be heard momentarily above the rattle of the Sniders, but they had no chance against the breech-loaders. As every puff of smoke blossomed, dozens of Sniders fired back and musketeer after musketeer tumbled back behind their rocks, riddled with bullets.

Napier then gave the order to halt. If the troops advanced too far before withdrawing for the night it might encourage Theodore to think that the British still feared him. The Kings Own stopped gratefully, conscious almost for the first time that they were very tired. Conscious too, suddenly, that it was pouring with rain which did much to allay their thirst. The sailors continued to bombard the retreating Abyssinians with rockets. A few of the enemy, with admirable persistence, attempted to slip round the right flank of the British but were soon driven off by a few steady volleys from the sappers and miners.

*　　*　　*

On the left the situation was more serious, and the fighting was for a time close and desperate. The mountain battery opened first with shrapnel, but a high proportion of the shells was defective and did not burst, so they switched, first to double common shell and then to case as the range shortened. Their fire, although accurate and effective, was not sufficiently intense to halt the Abyssinians who came on with great courage, leaving scores of dead behind them. The fierce pioneers, waiting impati-

141

ently until the enemy should be within effective range of their smoothbores, opened fire at a hundred yards, reloaded, delivered a second volley, and at once charged with the bayonet. There was a fierce and confused fight at close quarters for a few moments but the enemy, in spite of their numbers, were no match for the Sikhs hand-to-hand. They broke off the engagement and ran down the steep slope of the Dam Wanz Ravine, pursued by the exultant pioneers. There was no question of quarter; anything which moved was at once bayoneted and presently the slope of the ravine was covered with bloody corpses.

On the extreme left a great mob of Abyssinians continued to rush towards the baggage, still hopeful that they would have the chance to loot. As usual there was a shortage of muleteers so a great many of the 4th had been pressed into service as leaders. They did not hesitate. They were in no sort of order but they knew what to do. They dropped their lead ropes, unslung their rifles, and opened rapid independent fire at the charging enemy. The latter, finding that the innocent seeming baggage was, after all, extremely dangerous, stopped abruptly; the baggage guard then moved forward and under their fire the Abyssinians fled. The ravine was steep and narrow at that point so they did not spread out but ran back up the line of the King's road in a solid mass into which the riflemen continued to pour bullets as long as they could.

Even then the Abyssinians' ordeal was not over, for the bloodthirsty Sikhs had doubled over and were waiting expectantly along the lip of the ravine higher up. As the fleeing remnants of Theodore's army approached they swept down; the enemy took one look at the fierce, bearded faces and the bloodied bayonets and scattered desperately up the opposite slope like sheep, all thought of resistance gone. The mountain battery and the rockets continued to fire into the retreating Abyssinians until they had scrambled back wearily over the Fala saddle. Then the firing stopped and the battle of Arogi was over.

The first shots had been fired at about 16.00, the last at about 19.00—in the interval some two thousand of Theodore's unfortunate fighting men had been shot or bayoneted and his army crippled. The cost to the British was negligible; about twenty men were returned wounded, of whom two pioneers subsequently died and Captain Roberts of the Kings Own, who had commanded the baggage guard, received a serious wound which later cost him his left arm.

Thus it happened that the unexpected battle—provoked in part by a British tactical error—had proved decisive. On both the right and the extreme left the Snider had demonstrated very conclusively that the day of the muzzle-loading rifle was over, while in the centre the terrible Sikh pioneers had proved equally conclusively that the bayonet still had a place on the battlefield.

The quantity of ammunition expended had been extremely small for the effect obtained. The Kings Own fired ten thousand two hundred cartridges, or about twenty per rifle engaged, while the smoothbores of the Indian troops expended a further seven thousand eight hundred rounds—an average of perhaps seven or eight per musket. The mountain guns fired a hundred and two shells while the Naval Brigade used two hundred and nineteen rockets.

The proportion of Abyssinians killed or wounded by bullet, bayonet, rocket, or shell was never established (indeed the total casualties are to some extent conjectural, although they probably reached seven hundred killed and twice as many wounded) but it is certain that the ratio of casualties inflicted to rounds fired was extraordinarily high, and that the Snider in particular had more than proved its worth.

Theodore watched the battle from the gun positions on Fala and saw his army wither and die against the British fire and the Sikh bayonets. There was one brief moment of hope when the 4th Regiment halted and fell back to reform, and his courtiers began to shout excitedly that the British were retiring, but Theodore, watching through his excellent glass, knew better. His army was beaten.

Towards the end, as the weary remnants of his men climbed back up the slope, one of the naval rockets hissed past and killed a horse close behind him. The King was a brave man but the experience seemed to shake him. He shook his head,

143

commented sadly that it was a terrible weapon against which no man could fight, and then covered himself with his shield and remained silent.

Presently he stirred and began to call out for his chiefs, first for Fitaurari Gabri and then for other favourites, but as name after name elicited no reply he at last realized the full extent of the disaster. He stayed up on the Fala alone for many hours, wrapped in a cloak. Thunder rolled unceasingly above him, and below him he could see the torches flickering across the Arogi plateau as his people sought their dead. By midnight he had reached a decision. He summoned Flad and Waldemeier, both of whom he trusted, and sent them off to Magdala to find Rassam and say that he wished to open negotiations with the British Commander.

This done he retired to his tent where he turned to his old comforter, arrack, and was soon so drunk that when Flad and Waldemeier returned he at first abused them savagely. Then, in his strange erratic way he quietened down and from abusiveness changed swiftly to self-pity. The British, he said despairingly, had destroyed his whole army with their advance guard. What would they do when their whole force was present? What, he asked, should he do?

The two Europeans were in no doubt. They counselled peace, and after a brief pause he agreed. A few minutes later they were hastening back to Rassam with a message from the abject monarch that he would do whatever the envoy thought best.

19 A modern photograph of the great mortar 'Sebastopol', which still lies today, owing to its enormous weight, where it was toppled by the invaders. (*Stephen Bell & John Fynn*)

20 An Abyssinian mural depicting the events at Magdala. King
Theodore is in the top left hand corner, holding a revolver.
(Stephen Bell & John Fynn)

Theodorus, Emperor of Abyssinia

Sketched immediately after the capture
of Magdala. 13 April. 1868

by R. R. Holmes F.S.A
Archaeologist attached to
the Expedition

22 This old man is the grandson of Theodore's smith who made the shackles for his prisoners. A recent photograph. *(Stephen Bell & John Fynn)*

23 King Theodore's son Alamayu. After the death of his mother the British Government assumed responsibility for him, and he was brought up in England and educated at Rugby. He died at the age of eighteen without ever seeing his land again. *(Army Museums Ogilby Trust)*

24 The church at Magdala in which Theodore was buried.
(Army Museums Ogilby Trust)

25 The alleged site of Theodore's grave as it is today. *(Stephen Bell & John Fynn)*

26 On the top of Magdala, with Selassi rising in the background. *(Army Museums Ogilby Trust)*

27 10th Company Royal Engineers, Brevet-Major G. D. Pritchard commanding, after their return to Chatham. (*Royal Engineers' Museum, Chatham*)

CHAPTER 11

An Exchange of Letters

Tʜᴇ British camped on the field, the 1st Brigade on Arogi and the 2nd, which came up after the battle, at the head of the Warki-Waha Ravine. Everyone spent a miserable night, for it rained intermittently and as there were no tents the troops either slept uneasily on the wet ground or crouched round a host of dull, smoky fires, trying to warm themselves a little and dry their wet clothes. There was no shortage of food, for the men carried cooked meat and biscuits for two days, but water was scarce. The heavy rain had done a good deal to quench the thirst of the troops during the battle, and had also left small pools on the rocky ground although they were difficult to find in the darkness—except indeed when some exhausted soldier lay down in one.

Strong outposts were established round the camp for, apart from the normal tactical requirement of the situation, Theodore had a certain reputation for night attacks—many of the recent letters from the prisoners had warned Merewether that the King was boasting that he would destroy the British while they slept. In the event, no attack came. Theodore's concept of a swift rush in the dark was fundamentally sound, since in theory the darkness would have nullified the British superiority of fire. In practice, however, the Abyssinians might have had an unpleasant surprise, for although they could not know it Napier was prepared for a night battle. Part of the equipment brought from England by the British sapper company included three sets of

ᴋ

an early pattern searchlight. They had cost the considerable sum of three hundred and fifty pounds each, but were extremely effective, for they cast their beams a mile and a half and produced enough light for guns and rifles to shoot by. The engineers had set them up at intervals along the British front, so that Theodore's men were perhaps fortunate that they did not renew their attacks.

The night was, nevertheless, a disturbed one. Large numbers of Abyssinians came down with flaming torches to search for the bodies of their friends and relatives amongst the hundreds of corpses covering the field. They were afraid to come too close to the British outposts, but further out they were active all night and their voices, particularly those of the women, could be clearly heard in the British camp.

Even worse were the jackals and hyenas. They were plentiful in the vicinity of Magdala and now their hideous chorus echoed incessantly amongst the rocks, mingled with the despairing cries of the wounded.

*　　*　　*

By dawn next morning the British were busily engaged in making camp behind a strong line of Baluchi outposts. The bulk of the mules had come straggling in during the night, bringing food, ammunition, and a much needed supply of water, and preparations were being made for a hot meal after a wet and cheerless night in the open. While they were waiting for it the troop busied themselves cleaning their rifles, replenishing their ammunition from the reserve supplies brought up by the quartermasters, and generally preparing for a resumption of hostilities.

Daylight revealed the full horror of the battlefield. There were bodies everywhere, many in the open but a great number concealed in rocky crevices or patches of scrub, and the ground was splashed with trails of blood where badly wounded men had crawled painfully away to die. Everywhere too there were the horrid traces of the gruesome hyena feast of the previous night. Arrangements were at once put in train to count and bury the dead and find such wounded as still remained alive. A considerable number of these were brought in by the stretcher bearers to the British dressing stations and there dealt with by the surgeons, who were thus able to combine the demands of humanity with some excellent practical experience in dealing with gunshot wounds.

Many women were still searching hopelessly for sons or husbands and Captain Speedy sent up messages by some of these to say that all the dead and wounded might be removed without fear of British reprisals. The body of Fitaurari Gabri, the general who had led the Abyssinian attack, was soon found in its conspicuous shirt and cloak. A good many of the men of the Kings Own had not unnaturally believed him to be Theodore and he had attracted a great deal of fire. The dead men were therefore particularly thick around him, and included the bodies of seven lesser chiefs who apparently were attempting to remove his corpse when they too were struck down in turn.

The bulk of the dead were found on the left centre of the position where the Sikhs had delivered their charge in defence of the guns. No wounded were found there for the good reason that none had survived the bayonets of the pioneers, and the dead were heaped thick along the slopes of the Dam Wanz Ravine. The name meant in Amharic the Valley of the Dead and on this occasion the title was well justified. It was said that for a time after the battle, the little stream running down it had actually been stained with blood.

*   *   *

While the British were eating their breakfast some activity was observed on Fala and a rumour went round that another attack was imminent. All eyes turned to the steep hillside down which a small cavalcade could be seen riding cautiously. A dozen glasses were quickly focussed on the group, and soon disclosed not only a white flag, but also a red coat. Half an hour later Prideaux and Flad rode into camp on ornately equipped mules, accompanied by one Dejatch Alami, a relative and close confidant of Theodore.

They were given a wild greeting by the excited soldiery and a cheering crowd escorted them to the tent of the Commander-in-

147

Chief where General Napier was waiting to receive them. H. M. Stanley, who watched the scene, was astounded and impressed by the pains which Lieutenant Prideaux had obviously taken over his appearance. He was carefully shaved, his hair pomaded. his uniform spotless, and the whole effect was greatly enhanced in the eyes of the correspondent of the *New York Herald* by those almost indispensable items of kit of the British officer of the period—a monocle and a gold-knobbed cane.

After the first greetings, Prideaux wasted no time in delivering Theodore's verbal message that he acknowledged himself beaten and wished to be reconciled to the British. He then gave the Commander-in-Chief a good deal of enlightening information on Theodore's attitude and mental state.

The request put Sir Robert Napier in a difficult situation. He was in command of a rescue, not a punitive, expedition and strictly speaking it could be said that his object would have been fully achieved once the prisoners were safely in his hands. He had in fact employed the expression "overthrow Theodore" in his original memorandum to the Governor of Bombay, but this had presumably been used in the context of a fierce and pro- longed resistance by the King. This situation no longer existed, for Theodore was asking for terms. Blood had, however, been shed. Not very much on the British side to be sure, but enough to alter things.

There were a number of other important considerations. The entire operation had been facilitated—had indeed only been made possible—by the whole-hearted co-operation of the various princes and chiefs through whose territory the expedition had passed. These were all actively in arms against Theodore on their own account, and had made it clear that their co-operation was based on the double assumption that the British were first going to overthrow the King—and then quit the country. This had been the price of their help, and now it had to be exacted.

After some consideration the Commander-in-Chief dictated a message to Theodore:

Your Majesty has fought like a brave man and has been overcome by the superior power of the British Army.

It is my desire that no more blood may be shed. If, therefore, Your Majesty, will submit to the Queen of England
and bring all the Europeans in Your Majesty's hands and
deliver them safely this day in the British camp, I guarantee
honourable treatment for yourself and for all members of
Your Majesty's family.

* * *

While Napier was busy composing this letter the Abyssinian
member of the party was taken on a conducted tour of the
British Camp. He was shown the Armstrong guns, the eight inch
mortars, and the elephants which had carried them to Magdala,
and it was explained to him that these were vastly more powerful weapons than the mere toys with which the King's army
had been shattered on the previous day. It was also made clear
that failure on the part of Theodore to comply with Napier's
demands could only result in the complete destruction of the
King, his fortress, and the remnants of his army. Dejatch Alami
was suitably impressed. He had been present at the battle of
Arogi, and although a brave enough man the prospect of facing
these new and vastly more terrible weapons did not appeal to
him. He agreed honestly and whole-heartedly that there was no
apparent alternative between surrender and death, and in conversation let it slip that this also appeared to be Theodore's own
view. He added, however, that although the King might release
the prisoners unharmed he did not believe that he would ever
surrender his own person to anyone.

At the end of his tour the envoy said that he had been particularly instructed by Theodore to request permission to look
for the body of Gabri. He was informed that it had already been
found, was being treated with respect, and would be sent up to
the fortress as soon as a suitable opportunity presented itself, all
of which appeared to relieve him considerably.

When Napier's letter was ready, the party remounted its mules,
and rode back towards Fala. The feelings of the Europeans
cannot have been pleasant; Flad's wife was still a prisoner in the
fortress so that he had a considerable inducement to go back,

but it must have been a sad wrench for young Prideaux to leave the familiar atmosphere of the camp, and the companionship of his own kind to deliver himself back into the hands of the mad King. On his way through the outposts he confided quietly to Ensign Wynter of the 33rd that he had little hope of seeing the morrow, but he went on firmly, apparently undeterred by the fearful prospect which might be facing him at the summit of rock.

As soon as they were gone Napier began to doubt the wisdom of his action, and in particular about the wording of his letter. The success of the whole expedition was still very much in the balance, for Theodore still had the prisoners. If he took offence at the letter—or was drunk when it arrived—he might easily order their throats to be cut. He was quite capable of it; in certain moods he was capable of anything.

As it happened, his reception of the somewhat peremptory note might have been a great deal worse. He refused to accept the actual missive on the quaint ground that he did not wish to deal with any man who served a woman, but he listened attentively while its terms were interpreted and explained by Flad and Waldemeier, both of whom he trusted, and both of whom spoke Amharic well. Markham, in his account of the expedition, said that Theodore, "Never understood that he was expected to surrender his own person. No man would have dared to tell him so." There seems in fact to be little doubt that at least the possibility was made clear to him. He is reputed to have asked anxiously and repeatedly what Napier actually meant by "honourable treatment"; was he being offered assistance against his enemies, or a dignified imprisonment in exile? Prideaux must have known that the latter was intended, but he was understandably reluctant to make his opinion known. He sensibly refused to be drawn, and after much deliberation Theodore decided to address Napier again and ask for elucidation.

He at once dictated a long and rambling statement, the essence of which was that he acknowledged himself defeated but would not surrender his person, and as soon as it was ready Prideaux and Flad rode off with it to the British camp, apparently without reference to Rassam. Theodore then retired to his tent to pray and meditate, fortunately without the assistance of arrack.

After a while he called for some of his most trusted chiefs and asked their advice on the matter. The British were at his gate. What should he do? The chiefs were desperate men; fierce independent individuals who felt that they had little to hope for from the British, and even less from the rebels. It did not take them long to reach a conclusion, and all but two gave the same grim advice. Kill the prisoners, and fight to the end. One of those who disagreed was Dejatch Alami who had been in the British camp. He was a brave man but a realist, and he urged restraint. What, he asked, was the point of killing the prisoners? The British had come a long way at great trouble and expense to release them, and if they failed now at this late stage they would exact a terrible vengeance. It was clear that they had the power to do so; they had nearly destroyed the army with no more than a handful of men. Now their whole force was up with its great guns and mortars carried on elephants. What hope could there be of standing against them? Why die uselessly? Why not release the prisoners and send them down to the British camp? Perhaps that might even induce them to go away. Alami, a close confidant of the King, spoke with the authority of one who had seen the British force with his own eyes, and it is clear that his opinions reflected the King's own ideas on the subject.

Theodore was silent for a long time, then he ordered the British prisoners to be brought before him without saying what he proposed to do, and a party of soldiers went off to fetch them. As soon as they had gone the King fell into one of his sudden violent rages at the mere thought of surrender and decided that death by his own hand would be preferable. He drew a pistol from his belt, placed the muzzle in his mouth, and pulled the trigger, but the charge hung fire. His chiefs flung themselves on him, and there was an undignified scene while they all rolled on the ground together. During the course of this struggle the pistol actually went off without doing any damage, but the sound of the report brought the King to his senses. His rage abated as quickly as it had risen; he decided that fate had decreed that he should live, and at once lay down to sleep, having given orders that he was to be wakened when the captives arrived.

The feelings of the prisoners can be imagined. They had lived in hopes of release for months and years and it would be cruel to die with their rescuers almost within shouting distance.

The King and Rassam had a long talk. Theodore had always had an exaggerated idea of the envoy's importance, and had always believed him to be a man of vast influence in England, nor is it probable that Rassam did anything to undeceive him. Help was very close, but death was hovering over them and Rassam by that stage was probably prepared to say and promise almost anything for freedom. He was sure, he told Theodore, with more confidence than he probably felt, that he could soften Napier's demands. All that was required was a generous gesture on the part of the King to demonstrate his good faith—and what could be more suitable than the release of the prisoners?

Theodore agreed, and having made his decision seemed particularly keen for them to be on their way. Possibly he was only interested in pacifying Napier; possibly he did not trust himself in his sudden violent rages and was genuinely anxious for them to be out of his clutches before his mood changed. "Go," he said urgently to Rassam. "Go *NOW*. You can send for your baggage later."

They needed no urging and were quickly ready to leave. Theodore bade them farewell in the most affable manner, particularly Rassam of whom he appeared genuinely fond. Even the unfortunate Cameron, bent and twisted from torture, received a kindly word. They then mounted the mules provided for them and rode off, hardly daring to believe their luck. They were escorted by some of the artisans and by Dejatch Alami.

On their way down they met Prideaux and Flad riding slowly up the rocky road. Napier had refused to discuss matters further with Theodore and had simply sent them back with his original letter. The sight of Rassam and the others riding as free men to the British camp cheered them greatly. It looked after all as though Theodore was going to comply with Napier's demands;

they turned their mules thankfully and rode back with the others.

The party received a tremendous ovation in the British camp. General Merewether, who in many ways had been the man chiefly responsible for the whole expedition, had managed to smuggle some champagne forward for this very occasion, and it was now produced and the health of the ex-captives drunk. In general, they were in surprisingly good shape; Rassam excited and voluble, Dr Blanc cynical and calm. Worst off was Cameron whose long captivity and savage treatment had left their marks on him, but even he brightened when he found himself secure in the midst of a strong force of British and Indian infantry. That evening he and Kerens, his secretary, dined with General Napier, seated on the rocky ground and eating tough beef and chupattis, washed down with milkless, sugarless, tea. Both food and conditions were a good deal worse than they had enjoyed in Magdala, but the fact that it was their first meal in real freedom for several years probably more than made up for the shortcomings of the menu.

*　　*　　*

Back in Magdala, Theodore sent for Terunesh, his Queen. They had been estranged for some time and she had been living privately in her house in the fortress, but now she arrived with her six year old son, Theodore's only legitimate child, and they spent some time together, during which the King gave her detailed instructions regarding the future of the boy, whatever was to be his own fate.

He then sent for his scribe and dictated a second letter to Napier. It said nothing of his own surrender but was otherwise conciliatory in tone. In it he stated his firm intention to release all the prisoners, and in view of the fact that it was Easter Sunday begged his fellow Christian to accept an Easter present of a few cows.

It was despatched by the hand of one of his secretaries accompanied by a European artisan, and there is some doubt about its reception in the British Camp. The general consensus was that

153

Napier refused the gift categorically but Rassam, who acted as interpreter throughout, appears to have thought otherwise, and assured the secretary that it had been accepted. This, if true, was tantamount to saying that peace had been made, since by Abyssinian custom it was inconceivable that a general should accept such a present while still harbouring designs against the person of his opponent.

On his return the secretary was accompanied by Flad and the artisans who had escorted the prisoners down. The situation of the workmen was by no means clear. Technically, they were private employees of Theodore, and on consideration Napier thought it best to send them back to be properly discharged from the King's service. Most of them had left wives and families in Magdala, and were thus in any case anxious to return. They also carried back the body of Fitaurari Gabri, a gesture which touched Theodore and his chiefs, and impelled them to exclaim that the British were indeed true Christians.

On the way back the secretary, who rode with Flad, made no secret of his views on his master's future. When Flad, hearing that the cattle had been accepted, remarked cheerfully, "It is peace, then," the secretary replied bitterly "What does it matter to you whether it will be peace or not? Make haste and get away with your wife from the mountain. Would it not be as well if Theodore, who has oppressed us all, should be removed from Abyssinia?"

When they arrived with their message Theodore was delighted and at once sent off the present of a thousand cows and five hundred sheep. A little later he heard that they had been turned back at the British outposts and his spirits fell again. After considering the matter for a while, he apparently concluded that his peace offering had been refused because he still had the artisans and their families with him. He at once despatched the whole of them—men, women, and children—to the British camp and when they were out of his reach remarked hopefully to his attendants, "Surely it is peace, now that they have taken my power from me. Surely it is peace." He then withdrew all his guns from Fala and parked them on Islamgi, although it is not clear whether this was as a gesture of peace or in readiness for a possible withdrawal to a last ditch position in the main fortress.

*   *   *

The balance of the prisoners rode into the British camp on Arogi. As usual the word had got round and the troops, perhaps as much out of boredom as interest, crowded round to watch them arrive. They were a startlingly unanticipated group; almost all were either half-castes or full-blooded Abyssinians, and most of them wore native dress. The women also wore face veils, although the modesty of the custom was largely neutralized by the fact that they all rode astride. The only two European women amongst them were Mrs Flad and Mrs Rosenthal, both easily distinguished because they wore European dress and rode modestly on improvised side-saddles.

The officers put up their glasses in astonishment. The men crowded closer to watch. There was a deflating sense of anti-climax about the whole thing; had they really come all this way to release this strange caravan? All at once the humour of it struck the troops, and the puzzled ex-captives rode in to the accompaniment of great gusts of raucous laughter.

The total number released, including Rassam and the British Party, was fifty-nine, but on the morning after their arrival Mrs Moritz, wife of one of the artisans, brought it up to a round sixty by producing a son. It seemed appropriate to christen him Theodore.

*   *   *

Long after their arrival the cattle had still not been accepted, and Theodore at last realized that his gift had been refused and that he himself was in grave danger of falling into the hands of the British. He retired to Magdala with his attendants and spent a restless night.

Next morning was Easter Monday, 13th April 1868. At sunrise the King rose and assembled such of his troops as were available (about two thousand) and announced that he proposed to withdraw from Magdala and seek another refuge. Then he moved off south-east towards the Kaffir-bir Gate which led to the plateau of Sangallat, whence a path wound down into the valley. His men refused to follow. They were, they announced, tired of marching; they would fight and die at Magdala. Theodore turned wearily back up the hill. A few men would have undoubtedly gone with him, but Meer Akbir had done his work well. The Gallas were out in force on that side of the plateau, and it would have needed an army to fight a way through them.

On Islamgi the King halted and addressed his troops again. He told them that he himself intended to die fighting in Magdala, but that any man not wishing to stay with him could go. Perhaps to his surprise the offer was accepted. Immediately his army virtually disbanded itself and the soldiers spread uncertainly over the plateau, leaving Theodore with no more than the handful of chiefs and soldiers—perhaps a hundred altogether—prepared to stand by him.

While this was going on the British commander was making preparations to attack Magdala. He had received apparently authentic information that the Abyssinian army was fast recovering its morale after the shock of Arogi, and that many stragglers and lightly wounded men had rejoined the King. There seemed little point in waiting, and he gave order for his force to form up.

News then came in that Theodore had already gone, and this was confirmed by the appearance of a number of chiefs—previously loyal to him—who came down to surrender the fortress and asked for British protection. Some indeed requested that the country might be taken over and ruled permanently by them.

In view of this, Napier at once sent off messages to the Gallas offering them the enormous sum of fifty thousand dollars for the return of the King. He also deployed every cavalryman he had, including the newly arrived wing of the 3rd Dragoon Guards, along the foot of the western face of the fortress to head Theodore off if he tried to break out on the side. Even his little escort of twenty-five sabres was pressed into service, and young Scott, keen as ever, rode off with his handful of *sowars*, indulging on the way in vain daydreams of capturing Theodore.

Colonel Loch and Captain Speedy rode up the path to Fala

in order to open negotiations with the great mob of Theodore's disbanded army, and to clear them off the feature as far as possible so as not to hinder the attacking columns. They took with them an escort of fifty Indian cavalry, but met no opposition.

CHAPTER 12

The King Goes Down

DURING the approach march the 1st Division had been eche-loned back along the track, but now that it was concentrated on the Arogi Plateau for the final assault it made an impressive sight. The bulk of the force consisted of the two and a half battalions of British infantry. Most of their formal parade ground gloss was gone, but their brown bearded faces, their battered helmets, and their stained, ragged, khaki drill had a certain panache of their own, and they looked very ready to take Mag-dala. There were also the 1st Baluchis, steady and reliable, and the fierce Sikh pioneers, eager for another fight, one British and six Indian sapper companies, two companies of the 10th Bom-bay Native Infantry, and one mountain battery.

The remaining artillery, consisting of four Armstrong guns, two eight inch mortars, and the other mountain battery, were to remain at the foot of the ascent so as to be available to give supporting fire on to Selassi. There were no cavalry, the whole of that arm having been deployed as stops along the foot of the feature.

The advance began at about 08.30, and was led by the sappers carrying scaling ladders, the leading infantry battalion being the 33rd Duke of Wellington's. The path was steep and progress slow. The advance started in quarter-column but as Captain Hayward recalled,

> The ground became so rough that we had to form fours and move along Theodorus road which runs along the side

of Fala and is commanded by a plunging fire from Selassi. The road is tremendously steep and difficult in some places, and had Theodore opened up in the least we must have suffered a tremendous loss. . . . Well defended, it would have been impregnable and just the last part we had to climb upon our hands and knees up the face of the cliff, some 60 or 70 feet high.

The Abyssinians missed their chance, however, and the ascent was unopposed; a company of 1st Baluchis and the two of the 10th Native Infantry turned off to the right up the first suitable spurs and took possession of Fala, but the rest crawled slowly on. As they descended they were heartened to see thousands of Abyssinians, warriors, women, children, scrambling down the hill by every goat track, all making for asylum on the Arogi Plateau. Rumours came almost as thick. Theodore had flown. Theodore had shot himself. Theodore was massacring his political prisoners. Theodore was waiting at the top with ten thousand well armed men. Only time would tell the true situation.

Lieutenant Reeve of the 45th, anxious for glory, noted with some obvious disappointment that,

> As soon as I had scrambled to the top of the hill I found all the chiefs giving up their arms to General Merewether who was assisted by Mr Flad, one of the captives, and Mr Waldemar.

Action was still possible however because,

> There still remained the great stronghold of Magdala for us to take. . . . It was about three-quarters of a mile off, and standing completely by itself, appeared to be a massive lump of rock, and to the naked eye there was no apparent road to it. Down on the intervening plain we could see the 4th Kings Own lying down and a battery joining in. The principal object of their aim was the gateway.

At midday the head of the column scrambled onto the Fala saddle and began to work along it to Selassi, followed by the remainder of the force. The last few yards of the path were too steep for the heavily laden mules of the mountain battery but the determined gunners passed three guns up by hand and trundled them on behind the infantry.

Selassi was still crowded with Abyssinians, including hundreds of wounded from the Arogi battles, but although many of them were armed there was no resistance, and two companies of the 33rd began to shepherd them off the feature. It was necessarily a slow business because there were few practicable paths down, but eventually the summit was cleared. Immediately the Armstrong guns and mortars were brought up with great difficulty by the elephants, so as to be ready to provide support for the next phase.

While this was being effected Colonel Loch and Captain Speedy were making their way steadily forward along the feature further south. They met no opposition and the bulk of Abyssinians they encountered seemed favourably disposed and willing to accept Speedy's persuasive advice to evacuate the feature as quickly as they could. As the two officers reached the northern end of Islamgi, King Theodore and about a hundred followers appeared from the south and tried to carry off the guns parked there. The two parties faced each other for a while at long range and Theodore and some of his chiefs actually rode forward for some distance shouting taunts, firing their rifles, and calling out, Abyssinian fashion, for champions to be sent against them.

General Staveley saw this from further back and at once sent up a company of the 33rd in support, with orders to prevent the guns from being taken away. Two of the smaller pieces had already been removed by Theodore's men, but even at long range the steady fire of the Sniders proved effective and quickly drove the enemy back from the others. Loch and Speedy then advanced with the cavalry and took possession of the artillery. This was greeted by some ineffective small arms fire from Magdala, upon which Captain Speedy had the guns turned in that direction and fired. Theodore's men were still struggling frantically with the two they had succeeded in getting away, and although one or two shots from Speedy's impromptu discharge fell amongst them they would not abandon them. The company of the 33rd then doubled forward and as their shots began to take effect the Abyssinians finally gave up the struggle and left the guns to their enemies. They retired into Magdala and closed the gate firmly behind them.

General Napier then rode forward to reconnoitre the position, which at first sight seemed formidable. The bastion of Magdala rose some three hundred feet sheer above Islamgi, with only a single narrow path leading up to the gate. It was impossible to see inside, but constant movement indicated that it contained a good many people, and the occasional whiz of a musket-ball made it clear that some resistance was to be expected.

There was no point in wasting time. The Commander-in-Chief decided to shell the fortress and storm it out of hand, and at once gave orders for all available guns to be brought forward. Soon the mountain guns and naval rocket tubes were formed across Islamgi, some thirteen hundred yards from the gate, while the Armstrong guns and mortars were set up on Fala at almost double that range.

While the guns were being prepared some prowling officer happened to look over the precipice where Theodore's victims had been slaughtered a few days before, and presently a considerable number of others also visited the spot. It was a revolting sight, with heaps of hacked, bloated, hyena-torn corpses, and it made the troops more anxious than ever to get into Magdala and make an end of the place and its savage king as quickly as possible.

The guns opened fire at about 15.00 and continued for an hour. The ranges were rather long for accurate shooting but the top of Magdala was about three-quarters of a mile long and half a mile wide so that it was a difficult target to miss completely and shells were soon bursting among the hundreds of mat-huts covering the *amba*. There were in fact considerable numbers of people, including many women and children inside and some casualties were soon inflicted. Theodore watched with interest as the shells burst round him, until one fell so close that it killed one of his attendants. When this happened the King, who had always had enormous faith in the power and accuracy of well-handled artillery, concluded that the fire was being directed at him personally and went off to change his conspicuous clothing for a plain white linen cloak.

The infantry assault started at about four o'clock, and at that hour the Armstrong guns and mortars ceased fire, although the mountain guns continued in action. The nature of the ground made manœuvre almost impossible, so the plan was a simple one. Four companies of the 33rd Regiment were to advance as close as they could and then keep the gate, wall, and loopholes under rifle fire, while the remaining six companies under Major Cooper stormed it. A party of sappers was detailed to accompany the stormers and blow the gates if required.

The 33rd Regiment took their colours into action with them (and although no one present could know it, this was the last time they were ever to do so, for a few years later it was decided that the custom was out of place in modern war and in 1881 it was discontinued). Before the main body moved off the divisional commander rode up to the colour party and gave orders to the ensigns that once they were inside they were to signal success by waving the colours from the most conspicuous place they could find.

As soon as the four leading companies reached their positions they opened a heavy and accurate fire, under cover of which the stormers led off up the path. Puffs of smoke from the loopholes indicated some resistance but nothing could be heard above the incessant rattle of the Sniders from the support companies. The wing of the 45th Regiment was in immediate support, and moved behind the 33rd in quarter column.

The stormers, firing and cheering wildly, scrambled up the steep path and quickly reached the gate. This was of course locked and barred, and the hollow way behind it had been filled with hundreds of blocks of dressed stone by Theodore and his men so that the advance was checked at this point. A few casualties were incurred while the sappers were being called forward to blow the gate, but for the most part their defensive fire was easily subdued by that of the attackers.

A slight element of farce was then introduced into the proceedings by the discovery that the powder bags had been forgotten, and as the gate was obviously immovable by other means the commanding officer sent three companies along the wall to their right to see if they could find a way in. The wall was fronted by a thick thorn hedge but presently Private Bergin, an exceptionally tall and powerful man, found a thin place in this barrier and forced his way through. Drummer Magner, close behind him, then scrambled onto his shoulders and got his hands onto the top of the wall where he scrabbled helplessly for a few seconds until Bergin put the butt of his rifle under Magner's buttocks and with a vigorous thrust deposited him on top.

With his help Bergin, hoisted from below by his comrades, also negotiated the wall. He at once dropped onto the other side and opened a rapid, accurate fire at the handful of defenders until they retired within the inner gate, leaving several dead behind them.

Very soon Ensign Connor, Corporal Murphy and a number of other soldiers were over, and the position forced.

Young Wynter, although encumbered by the unwieldy regimental colour, had accompanied this detachment, and as soon as a few men were over the wall there was a great rush to get him forward to give the requisite signal to General Staveley. In spite of the steepness of the path and the weight of the colour he made good progress because as he commented later,

> I was hardly ever on my feet, as the men took me and the
> Colour in their arms and passed me from the centre to the
> front of the column. I shall never forget the exhilaration
> of that moment, the men firing and shouting like madmen.

He was soon on the wall, waving his colour wildly, to the accompaniment of a great outburst of cheering from below. A party then ran down and opened the main gate from the inside and the remainder of the stormers went pouring through.

Theodore and his handful of survivors had kept up a steady, though not very effective, fire as long as possible, but had then withdrawn through the inner gate. Here the King halted and released his followers from their allegiance. They had done as much as a handful of devoted men could be expected to do and he was generous enough to appreciate it and wish to give them a chance of life. They at once withdrew and dispersed over the *amba*, leaving the King alone.

The leading elements of the 33rd Regiment charged on up

the path over the scattered bodies, many of them victims of Private Bergin's accurate shooting, and through the second gate which had been left open. As they emerged on the other side they saw a single figure disappear behind a small stack of hay, and the scouts ran forward, rifles ready, to find a body lying on the ground, partly covered by a white cloak. They approached cautiously, bayonets lowered; all soldiers knew that wounded warriors had a habit of springing up at the last moment and laying about them frantically in a final desperate orgy of slaughter, and there was no point in taking chances.

They prodded the body cautiously, and when there was no reaction one of them turned it over with his toe. There was a gaping hole through the head and they relaxed, for it was clear that this particular warrior had fought his last fight. As the body rolled over, the cloak was drawn with it, and the movement revealed a handsome pistol. One of the soldiers bent and picked it up. This was better. Legitimate loot was always acceptable and although a pistol, even a good one, was not much use to the soldier, the young officers were always anxious for souvenirs and one of them would give him the price of a drink—perhaps the price of a drunk—for it. He turned it over carefully in his hands. There was a silver plate let into the butt, and he tilted it to the light and read the engraved inscription slowly:

Presented
by
VICTORIA
Queen of Great Britain and Ireland
to
THEODORUS
Emperor of Abyssinia
As a slight token of her gratitude
For his kindness to her servant PLOWDEN
1864

The 33rd Regiment had found King Theodore.

There was little more resistance. One or two irreconcilables fired a few shots at the advancing troops but a volley or two soon silenced them and it was all over. The *amba* was crowded with Abyssinians, all of whom had thrown away their arms and were hiding in the warren of huts.

Some, including the handful of defenders sent away by Theodore, had attempted to escape by the southern gate but had been driven back by taunting Gallas who by then were close up under the walls. As far as can be ascertained forty-five Abyssinians were killed by the 33rd in the assault; twenty more were killed, and a hundred and twenty wounded, by the preliminary shelling.

As soon as it was clear that resistance was over, the leading troops dispersed to plunder in the best traditions of the British Army at that time. There was a certain amount of attractive property lying about, and pockets were soon filled, but as far as the soldiers were concerned the great find was a considerable quantity of excellent arrack. They were mostly hard drinkers who had not tasted alcohol for some time, and they set to to repair the deficiency as quickly as possible. Magdala, however, was not to be a Badajos. The troops were kept firmly in hand, so that although there was some initial drunkenness it was soon checked, and no disorders occurred. Ensign Wynter's looting was confined to a cooked chicken, and a flask of *tej*, both very welcomed after his exertions with the colour, but he later bought a handsome silver mounted rhinoceros hide shield from his colour-sergeant for five dollars.

According to H. M. Stanley, the foremost amongst the plunderers were the missionary ex-prisoners whom he lumped collectively under the contemptuous title of the "black-coated gentlemen". They knew their way about the *amba*, and they wasted no time in making for the treasury and going carefully through its contents. One of the most unpleasant pieces of looting was the theft of a diamond cross from the body of the *Abuna*, the Patriarch of the Coptic church. He had been dead since October but had to await special rites before burial. His coffin was unceremoniously ripped open and the jewel taken.

As it happened little loot remained in private hands, for there was only one practicable way out of the fortress—through the northern gate—and that was firmly in the hands of the provost, backed by a guard of the 33rd Regiment. A few easily concealed items were undoubtedly smuggled through (including apparently the *Abuna's* cross, for it was never heard of again) and occasional exceptions were made in the case of bona-fide weapon trophies "taken at the point of the bayonet". The bulk of the plunder was handed over to a properly appointed prize master for disposal later. Amongst the most interesting and valuable items were the crown and royal seal of Theodore; these were taken possession of by General Napier in the name of Queen Victoria, with a view to their return when a new king emerged.

Even Theodore did not escape the souvenir hunters; his body was left exposed for some time, during which fragments of his clothing steadily disappeared until it was left practically naked. The corpse was then placed in a more secure situation. It had at first been thought that he had been killed by the 33rd but after some gruesome probing a post mortem decided beyond any doubt that the wound had been self-inflicted, as a Committee of Enquiry under Captain Johnson of the 33rd duly reported.

The Queen was found in her house in the fortress by the soldiers, and was at first treated with scant ceremony until she was eventually identified, and placed in the care of Captain Speedy. Napier consulted her as to the disposal of her husband's body, and she indicated that she would like it to be buried quietly in the church on Magdala. This was done the same day. No military honours were allowed, but a guard of the 33rd was present to keep order if required. There was no disturbance; the Abyssinian priests gabbled through their prayers without enthusiasm, the shallow grave was hastily filled in, and that was the end of Theodore, King of Kings, and Emperor of Abyssinia.

On 15th April, the 33rd Regiment was relieved in Magdala by the 4th, while the 45th was moved to Islamgi to guard the captured artillery and the great piles of rifles and guns, many of which were excellent percussion weapons of European manufacture. The 33rd had no regrets at leaving; the whole *amba* was in a foul and insanitary state, covered with the unburied carcases of animals and crawling with flies. They were only too pleased to leave it in the hands of their old friends and rivals of the Kings Own. The whole battalion was black with dirt and covered with fleas and everyone was glad of a chance to bathe in the Beshilo and wash off the worst of the grime and vermin.

The next question facing the British Commander-in-Chief was how to dispose of the thousands of Abyssinians who had been cleared off the main feature and concentrated on the lower plateau of Arogi. Magdala had been an outpost in Galla country and now they swarmed hungrily round the *amba*, a fierce, wild people, untidily festooned with the dried entrails of cattle which appeared to be their sole ornament, and eager for loot and vengeance.

One party even penetrated into Magdala itself, whence they were driven out by the British guard, while local stragglers were cut off and killed without compunction. The chances of the helpless, unarmed Abyssinians would have been slight indeed without the active protection of the British, who several times opened fire when the prowling Gallas became too persistent. On 15th and 16th April the problem was resolved by escorting the refugees across the Beshilo Ravine with strong cavalry patrols, which did not leave them until they were sufficiently far into Christian country to be reasonably safe from molestation.

The disposal of Magdala itself presented Napier with a problem. At first, anxious not to interfere with the balance of power in the country, he offered it to Wagshum Gobazi through his envoy, but that cautious ruler was not interested and refused it. Wagshum Gobazi commented sensibly that it would need a large garrison which he could not conveniently provide, and made it clear that as far as he was concerned the Beshilo was the natural boundary between himself and the Gallas.

The Gallas, on the contrary, laid strong claims to the *amba*, which they reckoned as part of their territory, but Napier was not disposed to agree. He therefore announced that he proposed to burn and otherwise destroy the place as far as possible as a mark of his Queen's anger at the ill-treatment by Theodore of the British prisoners, and once this decision had been reached preparations were put in train to implement it.

By the early afternoon of 17th April Magdala was deserted

except for guards and parties of sappers, and the work of destruction began. Twenty-six guns, the largest a forty-six pounder, were burst by enormous overcharges of powder (of which there was no shortage in the *amba*) and their carriages burned. Eight mortars were similarly destroyed but the last great piece, "Sebastopol", survived for the good reason that it was so short in the barrel and so wide in the bore that it would not burst. Its cart and base were burned and it was left lying in the wreckage, a vast and almost unmovable mass of brass.

The gates and other defences were mined with some of the huge quantities of powder and completely destroyed; then the palace, prison houses, and mat shelters were all fired. They burned steadily to the accompaniment of an incessant fusillade as thousands of stray shells and cartridges exploded in the flames, and a great pillar of oily black smoke rose for hundreds of feet over the rock to signal its destruction for miles around. The real strength of the fortress, however, was due to nature not art and could not be destroyed, so that as soon as the British, finally withdrew across the Beshilo on their return northwards the wild Gallas came swarming back and established themselves in triumph in the still smoking ruins.

*   *   *

The next few days were spent resting and reorganizing for the long return march. The General held a parade of the whole force at which he first congratulated it heartily on its achievements and then formally handed over the various European exprisoners into the care of the officers of their own nationalities who had accompanied the force as observers.

Once this was over the plunder taken at Magdala was put up for sale. Each unit present had been allowed to select a souvenir of the occasion, but apart from that everything was disposed of by public auction under the expert supervision of a Commissariat officer with experience in such affairs. Bidding was brisk, and so keen was the desire for mementos of the occasion that large prices were paid for rubbish. Mr Holmes of the British Museum, having ample funds at his disposal, bought a good many of the better items as did Colonel Fraser of the 11th Hussars who was buying for his mess, but a number of private buyers also laid out considerable sums. The total proceeds were over five thousand pounds and these were treated as prize money and distributed amongst the troops taking part. One item of particular interest which fell into British hands was the royal copy of the great book *Kebra Negast* (the *Glory of Kings*) which was a kind of Abyssinian Old Testament from which the rulers drew their authority. This item was also retained by General Napier and handed over to the British Museum on his return.

On 21st April a pioneer party marched northwards to ensure that the road was in good shape for the return of the main body. They also escorted a number of ex-prisoners, who had been released during the operations. Most of them were chiefs who had been detained by Theodore for political reasons, some for many years, and all were anxious to get home.

The march back, once started, went steadily. Now that the excitement was over the troops were feeling the strain of their prolonged exertions and monotonous diet, and the principal Medical Officer reported a marked increase in bowel complaints which he attributed to a lack of rum and sugar. Officially there was no scurvy, although some of the symptoms were apparent to Captain Hayward who on 15th April noted in his diary,

Cuts and bruises look angry and won't heal quickly. One's gums get sore and tender. In fact vegetables and cleanliness are requisite. We can't get sufficient water to wash our hands and faces every day and none of us have been able to wash our bodies since we halted at Dildi on 3rd April, nearly a fortnight ago.

The force was also by then very ragged and there was some increase in foot trouble, due in great measure to the seamed Indian socks. The weather too was bad, with a great deal of rain which increased the discomfort considerably, but in spite of everything morale remained high and the greatest number carried in *doolis* never exceeded eighty, which included the wounded.

It was at this stage that some disillusion regarding the prisoners first became apparent. They travelled with headquarters and Napier's ADC confided in one of his letters,

> I must say I think they are a queer lot, taken as a whole; the rag-tag and bob-tail they have with them in the shape of followers etc, are wonderful to behold. They have about twenty servants of each sort, and the idea of being able to move with less than three mules for baggage seemed to Mr Rassam as utterly impracticable. When the first night they came down and found we had no brandy, or cheroots, or rum, or anything of that sort to offer them, they seemed to think we were concealing them, (whereas we had had NO luxuries for the last month) and said if they had known it they would have brought their brandy and cheroots down with them! I have no doubt they have brought a lot of things with them in the way of business, now they are regularly settled and pitched in our camp, but they keep to themselves pretty well.

He did not actually add "Thank God" to his final phrase, but implied it very clearly.

*   *   *

There was trouble from the local tribesmen on the march back, particularly in the early stages. They had restrained themselves during the advance but now they became a considerable nuisance. There is something in the native mind which construes a return, even from a victorious and highly successful operation, as a retreat, and drives them to harrying tactics. Considerable bodies of both Abyssinians and Gallas assembled along the route and made repeated attempts to cut off stragglers and small parties of baggage. Once or twice they actually attacked armed soldiers but soon fled on realizing their mistake, and one or two postal *sowars* of the Indian cavalry were ambushed and killed for the sake of their horses and arms.

On the advance it had been possible to leave sick men and animals in depots along the route, but on the way back everything had to be swept up and carried back.

A permanent rear guard was established under Major Bray

of the 4th Kings Own, a competent and experienced soldier who had seen a great deal of service on the Afghan border. He was given wide powers and could put to death marauders caught red-handed, while two drummers were attached to him for the express purpose of inflicting corporal punishment if required. A great deal of trouble was caused by the weakness of the baggage animals. The bad weather made the track slippery and treacherous which particularly affected the camels, and many beasts were shot and their loads destroyed. So bad were the conditions that even the elephants began to weaken, and five of them had to be shot in the first few days.

The combined duties of whipping up straggling animals and beating off partial attacks from the bands hanging on the flanks were arduous, but Bray was well up to his task and made no mistakes. Napier often rode with the rearguard but never interfered with its handling.

If this was the orderly withdrawal of a victorious army through friendly country it is not difficult to imagine how the situation might have developed had the force sustained a reverse at Magdala. Fortunately things quickly improved; from Antalo northwards the march lay through the country of Prince Kasai who had remained steadfastly loyal. The death of Theodore had left him in as strong and secure position as any ruler could reasonably hope for in Abyssinia, and he appeared to be genuinely grateful for the part the British had played. There were no more raids, the path got better, and local purchase was much easier. As the force reached its various fortified posts along the way the supply situation also improved considerably. The first rum ration was issued between Dildi and Marwat, and thereafter half-forgotten luxuries began to reappear.

There was a short halt at Antalo where the force was reorganized and some changes made in the order of march. The 45th, who had already found marching with a brigade uncomfortable after their independent advance, were chagrined to find that they had been put even further back in the order of march. Their wait there was fortunately made bearable by an unexpected distribution of surplus medical comforts, and each officer received a bounty in the shape of a bottle of brandy, a bottle of port, a bottle of stout, some chocolate, and some meat extract. Markham summed up the joys of marching back along an established line of communication,

> But as the troops approached the base of operations their privations gradually decreased, and they came upon fresh luxuries at every march. Even commercial enterprise extended to within sight of Magdala itself, and a daring Greek arrived upon the Dalenta Plateau with Dutch cheese, boxes of sardines, and candles at fictitious prices. Rum appeared again and was heartily welcomed in Wadela; new boots and chocolate in Ashangi; damson jam, currant jelly, and mixed biscuits at Antalo; beer at Adigrat; and at Senafé there was a street of Parsee shops abounding in every kind of luxury!

*   *   *

On 30th April General Napier issued the following farewell order to the force:

Soldiers and Sailors of the Army of Abyssinia.
The Queen and people of England entrusted to you a very arduous and difficult task, to release British subjects from captivity, and to vindicate the honour of our Country which had been outraged by Theodore, King of Abyssinia.
I congratulate you with all my heart on the noble way in which you have fulfilled the commands of our Sovereign.
You have traversed, often under a tropical sun or amidst storms of rain and sleet, four hundred miles of mountainous and rugged country—you have crossed ranges of mountains—many steep and precipitous, more than 10,000 feet in altitude, where your supplies could not keep pace with you. In four days you passed the formidable chasms of the Beshilo, and when within reach of your enemy, though with scanty food, and, some of you, even for many hours without either food or water, you defeated the army of Theodore which poured down upon you from its lofty fortress in full confidence of victory.
A host of many thousands have laid down their arms at your feet. You have captured and destroyed upwards of thirty pieces of artillery, many of great weight and efficiency, with ample stores of ammunition. You have stormed the

almost inaccessible fortress of Magdala, defended by Theodore and a desperate remnant of his chiefs and followers. After you forced the entrance to his fortress, Theodore, who himself never showed mercy, distrusted the offer of it held out to him by me and died by his own hand. You have released, not only the British captives, but those of other friendly nations. You have unloosed the chains of more than ninety of the principal chiefs of Abyssinia. Magdala, on which so many victims have been slaughtered, has been committed to the flames and now remains only a scorched rock.

Our complete and rapid success is due, firstly, to the mercy of God, whose hand, I feel assured, has been over us in a just cause; secondly, to the right spirit with which you have been inspired.

Indian soldiers have forgotten the prejudices of race and creed to keep pace with their European comrades. Never did an army enter on a war with more honourable feelings than yours; this it is that has carried you through so many fatigues and difficulties; your sole anxiety has been for the moment to arrive when you could close with your enemy. The remembrance of your privations will pass away quickly; your gallant exploits will live in History.

The Queen and the people of England will appreciate and acknowledge your services; on my part, as your Commander, I thank you for your devotion to your duty, and the good discipline you have maintained throughout. Not a single complaint has been made against a soldier of fields injured or villagers wilfully molested, either in person or property.

We must not, however, forget what we owe to our comrades who have been labouring for us in the sultry climate of Zula, the Pass of Kumayli, or in the monotony of the ports which maintained our communications. One and all would have given anything they possessed to be with us—they deserve our gratitude.

I shall watch over your safety to the moment of your re-embarkation, and shall to the end of my life remember with pride that I have commanded you.

A day's march north of Antalo Queen Terunesh died. She had had consumption for some time and although the medical officers with the force did all they could they were unable to save her. She was buried by the Abyssinian priests with all ceremony, the cortége being led by the band of the Kings Own playing the *Dead March in Saul*, and accompanied by a guard of honour of the same regiment. It was one of those unusual duties which the British Army has always taken in its stride.

On 24th May at Senafé the Commander-in-Chief held a review of all available troops in honour of Queen Victoria's birthday. Prince Kasai was present as a guest and the next day there was a *durbar* at which Napier made him the considerable gift of eight hundred and fifty percussion muskets—part of those withdrawn when some of the Indian troops had taken over the discarded Enfields of the 33rd. The present also included a large quantity of powder and ball, together with the promise of six mortars and six light howitzers for which Napier had sent to India. The reward was well-deserved, since without Kasai's active co-operation the march to Magdala would hardly have been possible. Napier admonished him solemnly to use the weapons for defensive purposes only.

Five days later the last of the British troops had left Senafé and were on their way down the pass. The early and unexpectedly heavy rains had done a good deal of damage to the ramp at Suru and a number of followers and animals had already been overwhelmed and drowned in the sudden torrents which filled the narrow pass after a downpour. Stanley, anxious to depart now that the operations were over, was caught in such a deluge and only managed to escape by scrambling with his party onto a huge, flat rock. There they sat disconsolately watching corpses, carcases, bullock carts, telegraph poles, and bales of forage go rolling past in the sudden flood and wondering if their own persons would shortly be added to the sad debris. Fortunately the rain stopped when the water level was only an inch or two below their refuge, and in an hour the pass was dry again.

In its last few days in the country the force suffered a loss in the person of Mr Dufton, the Abyssinian explorer, who had done a good deal of useful work in his quiet, unobtrusive way. Although there were strict orders against individuals moving without an escort he had chosen to ignore them, perhaps thinking that he was sufficiently well known to the locals to be safe. He was wrong. A wandering band of Shohos robbed and murdered him.

A party of Indian troops at once set out after them, apparently guided by a prisoner whom General Merewether believed knew something about the affair. They actually found some property which had belonged to Dufton and later located a party of Shohos. These promptly fled up the mountain side, whence they rolled huge boulders down at the soldiers, and as they were far too active to be caught on their own ground the chase was abandoned. According to the subsequent report on the affair by the commanding officer the prisoner attempted to escape in the confusion and was promptly shot.

On his return to Zula, Sir Robert Napier took the unusual step of sending home his dispatch with one of the base staff rather than with an officer who had actually been to Magdala. He did this to indicate his satisfaction at the way the various administrative arrangements had been carried out, and his choice fell on Major Frederick Sleigh Roberts. Base administration was not in the least the sort of thing likely to appeal to an officer of his calibre, the holder of the Victoria Cross and a future Field-Marshal, and it is clear that he had thoroughly disliked every minute of his stay in Zula. Nevertheless he was an officer of great capacity and there is little doubt that much of the smooth running of the base had been due to his efforts. Roberts set off at once and was in England in three weeks. He at first took the dispatch to the Secretary of State for India but that individual, after reading it, sent him on with it to the Duke of Cambridge. When he arrived at Gloucester House Roberts found the Duke in the middle of a dinner party, and therefore left the dispatch and his visiting card with a footman and went modestly off to his club. An ADC was sent after him *post haste* and he was conducted back to receive a warm welcome from the Duke and his guests, amongst whom were the Prince and Princess of Wales.

By 10 June re-embarkation was complete except for a small rear party and on that day General Napier sailed for England. The bulk of the force returned to India, but British units which had completed their tour were sent straight home. The 33rd Duke of Wellington's went back via Suez and arrived in Portsmouth to a tumultuous welcome.

The disposal of the vast quantities of equipment and installations at Zula caused some trouble. As much as possible was sent back to India, but the heavier items—the railway and certain buildings included, were handed over to the Egyptians in Massawa. Considerable quantities of food and forage and various odd items of stores were given to locals, and in a few days the once busy port was dismantled and deserted.

POSTSCRIPT

The success of the expedition roused great enthusiasm in England, not only because honour had been satisfied, but also because the post-Crimean reforms in the army had apparently been justified in the clearest possible way. The fact that it was not strictly a British Army affair in the sense that it had not been launched or directly supervised by the War Office was hardly relevant. As far as the public, and indeed the nations of Europe, were concerned it had been a British expedition, led by a British general in which British soldiers (who seem to have had the lion's share of the publicity,) had triumphed over a host of difficulties and dangers.

The Duke of Cambridge was particularly delighted. He at least had never doubted the eventual success of the operation, and as early as November 1867 he had written to Napier to say that,

> The English papers have, I think, been writing very foolishly as regards this war. No doubt it will be a difficult operation, and it cannot be denied that we know little or nothing of the country in which our troops are to operate, but I have no idea that the difficulties are likely to turn out insurmountable. . . .

Now his faith was justified and he was able to write delightedly, quoting Wellington, of his pride in an army which could go anywhere and do anything.

The Queen at once expressed her great pleasure. Other messages of congratulations poured in. All was light.

M   177

There can be little doubt that the expedition marked a new level of efficiency in British military affairs, a fact not lost on Britain's European neighbours. Its success also impressed itself on a number of lesser dignitaries. It was a good thing for the rulers of an Empire to give an occasional demonstration of the length of their arm and this had been done sufficiently convincingly for Stanley to write of the expedition that "Princes and potentates scattered far apace heard the noise of it and trembled."

Some of its popularity at least was due to its impartiality. It had been a police action, necessary and justified, and once it was over the British had withdrawn swiftly without making any claims, territorial or otherwise, on the country.

It seems certain that the Abyssinians themselves were astonished. According to Waldmeier (who knew them well),

> The people of Abyssinia were astounded that the English left the country to itself and did not take possession or even nominate a Government for it. . . . In future, however, I feel that some European country will exert its dominion over that healthy, fertile country.

Honours and awards rained down; Napier became a peer. Major-General Malcolm who had commanded the lines of communication and Captain Heath, RN, the Senior Naval Officer were knighted. Staveley, already a Knight Commander of the Bath, was promoted substantive Major-General, his previous rank having been local only. No less than twenty-six others became Companions of the Bath, several were appointed as aides-de-camp to the Queen, and there were numerous brevet-promotions. Private Bergin and Drummer Magner both received the Victoria Cross, being the first members of the 33rd Regiment to do so, and there were a number of lesser awards.

A campaign medal was struck and issued to all troops taking part; a circular silver piece bearing the head of Queen Victoria within a nine-pointed star, and between the points were the letters A.B.Y.S.S.I.N.I.A. It was unique in that those awarded to British troops bore the name of the recipient in raised letters on the reverse, a distinctive plan but a very expensive one since it involved the preparation of a separate die for the reverse of each piece. Medals given to Indian troops were engraved in the usual way, and in all cases the piece was suspended from a rather wide red ribbon with white edges. Battle honours were awarded to all regiments taking part, even those which had not heard a shot fired.

* * *

As it happened the campaign set a fashion for remote, pioneer-type operations, since it was followed in fairly quick succession by expeditions to Western Canada, Ashanti, South Africa, Zulu-land, Afghanistan, the Sudan, and Burma, all of which bore some similarity to Napier's operation as far as the problems of move-ment and supply were concerned.

In spite of their valuable experience, few of the participants in the Abyssinian campaign achieved any great distinction in these or later campaigns. Roberts of course became a household name and Lord Chelmsford, who as Colonel Thesiger had been Napier's Assistant Adjutant-General, commanded the British forces successfully (though somewhat unconvincingly) in Zulu-land, but most of the plums fell to Wolseley and his protégés.

Of the senior officers, Napier became Commander-in-Chief in India in 1870 and remained in that capacity until 1876 when he became Governor of Gibraltar. He retired in 1879 with the rank of Field-Marshal and was Constable of the Tower from 1886 until his death in 1889.

General Staveley commanded the Western District in the United Kingdom from 1869 until 1874 and was then Commander-in-Chief Bombay until 1878. He became a full general in 1887 and died in 1896.

Merewether, who had been appointed to the command in Sind in 1867, finally took up his appointment in 1868 and retained it until his retirement eight years later; he died in 1880.

The energetic Phayre soldiered on in India. He became a general in 1877 and was promoted steadily through the various grades of the Bath, finally attaining the GCB in 1894, three years before he died.

Of the principal civilian actors in the drama, Cameron, worn out by his ill-treatment at the hands of Theodore, died in 1870.

Rassam, his fellow captive, had better fortune. He resigned his Aden appointment in 1868 and married an English wife; then in 1876, assisted by Layard, he resumed archaeological excavations in the Middle East until he finally retired to Brighton in 1882. Thereafter he spent his time writing books on archaeology and religion and, having been converted to evangelical views, had frequent brushes with the High Church. He suffered some ill-health as a result of his Abyssinian ordeal but neverthless survived to the age of eighty-four, dying in 1910.

Saddest of all perhaps was the fate of Theodore's son. After the death of his mother the British Government assumed responsibility for him, and he was brought up in England and educated at Rugby. He died at the age of eighteen without ever seeing his own land again and was buried in St George's Chapel, Windsor.

*   *   *

Once the initial spate of congratulations was over some of the gilt was scraped from the gingerbread by the realization that the expedition had cost the public nearly nine million pounds instead of the much smaller sum which Mr Disraeli had so confidently predicted.

This caused an immediate uproar in Parliament and a Select Committee was set up to report on the whole financial aspect of the campaign, which meant virtually the whole expedition. The matter was examined in great detail (the report ran to nearly seven hundred pages of small print) and a great deal of interesting information emerged.

It was established that by far the greatest item of expenditure had been the chartering of shipping. Vast tonnages had been employed, often at very high rates, so that the cost of that one item alone had been in the region of three and a half million pounds, which did not include money expended on the actual purchase of lighters and other shallow draught vessels for use in Annesley Bay. One case on which the committee commented was the expense of the hospital ships. Although it had been generally thought that old line-of-battle ships could have been converted cheaply for the purpose, three civilian vessels had in fact been used. It is an indication of the profits made that the cost of charter amounted to a hundred and thirty-five thousand pounds for these three ships, which at the end of the expedition were sold for a total of fifty thousand pounds!

It was clear that extremely high rates had been paid and that the most economical use had not always been made of the vessels available. This was to a great extent due to the lack of communication. There was no submarine cable to Bombay or even to Suez, so that it had been impossible to stop or change the course of ships once they had sailed.

The next largest expenditure had undoubtedly been the land transport. The problems connected with this have already been discussed in some detail and there is no point in repeating them, but it was considered that there had been an unnecessarily high expenditure due to the hasty and *ad hoc* arrangements which had had to be made. It was calculated that after allowance had been made for shipping and forage, each beast had cost an average of fifty pounds by the time it was put ashore at Annesley Bay, and the wastage had been enormous. A total of twenty-eight thousand six hundred and seventy-three animals of various species either died or were destroyed or abandoned in the course of the operations, which alone accounted for about a million and a half pounds. Among the hired animals, camels in particular had foundered, due in many cases to the fact that unscrupulous contractors had provided sick or immature beasts in the first place. Over four thousand unsatisfactory muleteers, most of whom hardly did a day's work, also had to be paid off and returned to their countries of origin.

Other wastage was due to over-insurance in the matter of food and forage. It will be remembered that Napier had originally planned to be completely independent of local supply and had calculated on establishing a six months' reserve. By the time it had become clear that this was not possible because of the difficulties of land transport, it was too late to cancel the considerable quantities already dispatched, and some ships lay for months in Annesley Bay loaded with forage which was subsequently destroyed.

Other errors occurred because shipments of stores from India were sometimes duplicated by similar cargoes from the United Kingdom, again due mainly to poor communications. One splendid, if minor, example came to light when it was discovered that thirty-eight tons of rice and sugar had actually been sent to India by the home authorities for use on the expedition.

Another heavy but unavoidable item of expenditure had been incurred in the provisions of some hundred thousand tons of coal for the condensers at a cost of up to seven pounds per ton, while one million three hundred thousand pounds had been spent on local purchase in Abyssinia.

Some criticisms were voiced of various increases made in the size of the force by Napier after his initial estimate. In view of the extended nature of his lines of communication, he had originally decided that he would prefer a relatively larger number of weaker units for the sake of flexibility, and had therefore calculated his numbers on the basis of peacetime strengths. Owing to a misunderstanding, most units had been made up to establishment by drafting, which added appreciably to the overall total. The Coolie Corps, a later and most useful addition, was also the subject of some discussion.

In fact heavy expenditure was probably inevitable, for there were no precedents on which to base even a rough estimate of the probable cost. One of the causes of the subsequent uproar had undoubtedly been Mr Disraeli's unwise confidence in even the approximate accuracy of the original calculation. Had he frankly admitted the lack of data on which to work and asked for an initial appropriation of, say, five million pounds without prejudice to further requirements, Parliament might have blenched but they were too deeply committed to have refused.

One interesting and justified objection was that once the Government had decided on the expedition it had abdicated all responsibility by giving General Napier *carte blanche*. The General was a soldier, not a financier, and his sole interest had been to ensure the success of the operation without bothering much about the probable cost.

Some comment was made on the lack of business instinct in soldiers. This was denied by nobody, least of all the soldiers themselves, few of whom wished to be tainted by any connection with trade. It so happened, however, that at the very time the committee was sitting, a new department was in process of being set up by the War Office as part of the wider army reforms. This was the "Control" department, the function of which was to control and co-ordinate the activities of all the so-called "spending" departments of the army. It was staffed in the main by specialist officers who were not too proud to deal with such sordid matters as finance.

In the event, the finding of the committee was mild. A good deal of money had been spent, some of which had been wasted, but the expedition *had* worked. The rulers of Europe had been impressed and lesser, more remote, potentates provided with considerable food for thought. The very success of the operation was great enough to cloak departmental and administrative shortcomings, a fact made amply clear by the two final paragraphs of the report:

15. That looking to all the circumstances attending the preparations for, and the conduct of, this most remarkable and signally successful expedition, your Committee, while pointing, as they have done, to what appears to them instances of defective organization and insufficient control over the expenditure of public money, bear ready testimony to the zeal and energy of all concerned, by which the Expedition was carried to so successful a conclusion.
16. That looking also to the privations which our troops suffered in the Crimea through defective transport and supplies, culpability amounting to crime would have attached to those charged with the conduct of the Expedition, whether at Home or in India, if the troops engaged had suffered, or the success of the undertaking had been endangered, and the lives of the prisoners had consequently been sacrificed for these causes.

Looking back on the expedition after the lapse of a hundred years there is little doubt that it was a remarkable, if expensive, piece of planning and execution. Apart from the somewhat peculiar handling of the reconnaissance in force over the Beshilo to Arogi, it is difficult to detect any major error or omission on the part of Napier. The most serious miscalculation was made over the initial size and organization of the transport corps, but in this Napier had no hand. He had indeed seen from the first that it would not work, and it is greatly to his credit that the *ad hoc* arrangements subsequently made by him worked so well. The deficiencies of his own organization drove him to rely on local supply and local transport more than he had ever thought desirable, or even possible. He had nevertheless considered the potentialities in his original appreciation which had also assessed with great accuracy the probable reaction of the Abyssinians as a whole.

The only element of luck came in something which no man could foresee; the reactions of Theodore. Here indeed things turned out fortunately. Had the King chosen to move away from Magdala, taking the prisoners with him, the operations would probably have degenerated into a hopeless pursuit, ending in failure. Had he gone without them they could of course have been released fairly easily and Napier's original object thus achieved, although the chiefs who had been so co-operative would have undoubtedly felt betrayed by a tame ending, and might well have turned against him.

The real stroke of tactical fortune was undoubtedly Theodore's wild attack at Arogi which destroyed half his army and shattered the morale of the rest without the slightest advantage to his cause.

Theodore had been a good soldier in his day and obviously had a fairly wide, if necessarily theoretical, knowledge of the capacity of a modern European army, so that his attack was literally that of a mad man, although by all accounts his men were equally anxious to go. The British were to some extent caught off balance but their superiority of firepower and discipline left them such a wide margin that there was never any real possibility of defeat, although with more planning, Theodore's men might have achieved some local success against the guns and baggage. It is a fair criticism of Napier to say that he exposed himself to a battle at a time when only one of his two and a half British battalions were available to fight it, but this can as fairly be answered by the simple, final test of any battle. He won decisively.

The real point on which it is interesting to speculate is what would have happened if a more balanced mind had been in command of the Abyssinians. Magdala was a position of extraordinary natural strength; its main weakness from the point of view of a prolonged resistance was its lack of water, but as the British could not have hoped to establish a close line of circumvallation, even aided by the Gallas, it is likely that adequate supplies could have been obtained by the defenders. Nor would the British have been able to invest Magdala; lack of material, munitions, and supplies of all kinds made it impossible. An absolute repulse was perhaps unlikely, but the approaches to the place were steep and difficult and a few hundred men armed with good percussion guns (of which there was no shortage) and backed by a formidable, if poorly handled, artillery, might have made its capture an extremely costly business.

Napier at least had no doubts of his good fortune; he told the Committee that,

> The only means of approach ran round the sides of this hill [Fala]; if simply old women had been at the top, and hiding themselves behind the brow had thrown down stones, they would have caused any force a serious loss. Had Theodore not thrown away his position by launching his Army against us, we could not have taken the position from him except at a very serious loss.

The very success of the expedition tends to screen its potentially desperate nature. Many things could have gone wrong and converted a triumph into a terrible disaster. Napier, in his address to the force at the conclusion of the campaign, attributed the success to "the mercy of God whose hand, I feel assured, has been over us,"—which may be as good a reason as any.

*   *   *

After a long internal struggle for power Theodore was finally succeeded in 1872 by the Prince of Tigré. One of his first acts was to request the return of the royal copy of the *Kebra Negast* for the odd but quite credible reason that his people would not obey him unless it was in his possession; it is to the credit of the British Government that it was promptly returned.

The country never sank back into its earlier isolation. Various nations had designs on Abyssinia and although an Egyptian attempt at invasion was repelled comparatively easily, the Italians proved to be more formidable opponents until disaster struck them. Their somewhat inept attempts at peaceful penetration having failed, it was decided to resort to open force to settle the problem, and in 1896 an Italian Army of some 14,500 men attacked Adowa. Everything however went wrong.

The plan of campaign was over-elaborate. The various columns came into action piecemeal, and the Abyssinians, united for once in the face of such a grave external threat, won an overwhelming victory. Eight thousand Italians and four thousand of their native troops were killed, and nearly two thousand captured. Only a handful succeeded in escaping back up the passes.

This decisive defeat of a European army, if only a third rate one, brought Abyssinia into prominence, and there followed a steady influx of Europeans into the country. Menelik, the new Emperor, saw the need for some degree of modernization and encouraged the opening of trade routes and the construction of railways, and although the Great War gave the country a brief respite from this relentless westernization it was quickly resumed in 1919.

In 1930 Ras Tafari was crowned Emperor. He had some knowledge of Europe, and had in fact visited England in 1925 to receive Theodore's crown from the hands of King George V. Ras Tafari was in favour of progress too, and had every intention of leading his country forward into the twentieth century, but in this he was thwarted by Italy. The rise of Mussolini and his fascist regime caused a great desire for colonial expansion, and Abyssinia was almost the last country available for such dubious attentions. A success there would not only consolidate an African empire, but would wipe out the forty year old disgrace of Adowa. In 1935 the Italians invaded.

The fact that Abyssinia had been a fellow member of the

League of Nations since 1923 meant nothing. Mussolini said brusquely that the Abyssinians were unfit to rule themselves and continued his operations unimpeded by the rest of the world. After heavy fighting, his modern weapons (particularly his aircraft) turned the scales; Abyssinia became an Italian colony, and its Emperor sought asylum in England. The country was never fully subjugated, and by 1941 its independence had been regained with British assistance and Haile Selassie restored to the throne which he still occupies.

List of Units Taking Part

Cavalry

HQ Wing, 3rd Dragoon Guards	Lt.-Col. C. Tower
10th Regt Bengal Native Cavalry (Lancers)	Major C. H. Palliser
12th Regt Bengal Native Cavalry (Lancers)	Major H. H. Gough, VC
3rd Regt Bombay Native Cavalry	Lt.-Col. J. C. Graves
3rd Regt Sind Horse	Major W. C. Briggs

Artillery

2 Rocket Batteries, Naval Brigade	Commander T. B. H. Fellowes, RN
G Battery 14th Brigade Royal Artillery (Armstrong Guns)	Captain A. H. Murray, RA
No 3 Battery 21st Brigade Royal Artillery, with Mountain Train	Captain (Brevet Lt.-Col.) L. W. Penn, RA
No 5 Battery 21st Brigade Royal Artillery, with Mountain Train	Captain G. Twiss, RA
No 5 Battery 25th Brigade Royal Artillery with Mountain Train	Captain (Brevet Major) A. H. Bogle, RA
No 1 Company, Native Artillery	Captain (local Major) P. D. Marrett, RA

Engineers

10th Company Royal Engineers	2nd Captain (Brevet Major) G. D. Pritchard, RE
4 Companies Bombay Sappers & Miners	2nd Captain A. T. Macdonnell, RE
3 Companies Madras Sappers & Miners	2nd Captain (Brevet Major) N. D. Prendergast, VC, RE

Infantry

1st Bn 4th Foot (Kings Own Royal Regiment)	Major (Brevet Lt.-Col.) W. C. Cameron

189

26th Foot (Cameronians)	Lt.-Col. S. Henning
33rd Foot (Duke of Wellington's)	Colonel A. R. Dunn, VC (followed by Cooper)
45th Foot (Sherwood Foresters)	Lt.-Col. W. H. Parrish
21st (Punjab) Bengal Native Infantry	Major J. B. Thelwell, CB
23rd (Punjab) Bengal Native Infantry (Pioneers)	Major C. F. Chamberlain
2nd Bombay Native Infantry (Grenadiers)	Lt.-Col. St. J. O. Muter
3rd Bombay Native Infantry	Lt.-Col. E. Campbell
5th Bombay Native Infantry (Light Infantry)	Lt.-Col. W. Taylor
8th Bombay Native Infantry	Lt.-Col. J. P. Sandwith
10th Bombay Native Infantry	Lt.-Col. J. Field
18th Bombay Native Infantry	Lt.-Col. J. J. Coombe
25th Bombay Native Infantry (Light Infantry)	Lt.-Col. A. B. Little
27th Bombay Native Infantry (1st Baluchi's)	Major H. Beville
1 Company 21st Bombay Native Infantry (Marine)	Lt. T. Beck

Note: The brevet rank held by several of the officers listed above was given to outstanding individuals as a means of accelerating their military progress.

Brevet rank applied in the Army as a whole, but was disregarded regimentally, so that the holder did duty and took precedence in his substantive rank while serving with a unit. This could lead to odd situations; for example, Major (brevet lieutenant-colonel) X might be the junior of the two majors in his battalion and yet senior by brevet to all the lieutenant-colonels in the brigade, including his own commanding officer. If, in such a case, his commanding officer was absent from duty, Major Y, the senior major, automatically assumed command by virtue of his *regimental* seniority; but if the brigade commander was away, Major X assumed command of the brigade by virtue of his *army* seniority, the brigade being classed as "the army as a whole".

Memorandum by the Commander-in-Chief of the Bombay Army

September 6th, 1867.

The expedition will consist of a force that may be stated in round numbers: 4,000 British, 8,000 native troops; with at least an equal number of camp followers, and 25,000 head of cattle of various kinds.

All of these cannot arrive at once, but it will be well to assume that one-fourth of the number may arrive together or within very short intervals.

It is probable that as many as 150 transports may be assembled at one time.

Points requiring attention

A good harbour or roadstead.

A good shore for landing.

A plentiful supply of good water as near the beach as possible, and a report, as far as ascertainable, of its quality at all seasons.

A convenient, healthy locality, for the depot of stores on first landing, to be called Post No 1, with room for the sheds, encampment of troops, picketing of horses and other animals, immediately after their being landed, and pending their removal to a greater distance.

A suitable situation for the camp of the troops to protect the depot on shore.

A position, which will not interfere with the encampment of the troops, for the encampment of the native followers who will probably collect and remain during the expedition, as well as those who may merely halt on their way with the force.

A position for collecting and organizing the land transport for the force as it is gradually landed, where large numbers of cattle can be picketed, fed, and watered; also herded for pasture in the day.

It is certain that there will be required some protection for the cattle thus collected up to the time that the advanced brigade is established at a Post No 2 on the highland, and even subsequent to that time, and that a force of perhaps a regiment of cavalry, and one of infantry, may remain there for some weeks.

The nearer that this spot is to the landing-place, the greater will be the facility of supplying all stores and equipments.

It is also to be taken into consideration that, if the above spot should be found near the coast, it may be necessary to seek for an encampment for the British troops at a higher elevation, in case they should be detained for some time before it was found convenient to move on to the tableland.

An elevated healthy spot should be looked for; the situation of this place would depend upon the existence of abundant natural forage, water and salubrity.

The foregoing conditions are very important, if not indispensable.

It is to be hoped the reconnoitring party may succeed in obtaining them at a point of the sea-shore which will give the shortest approach to the healthy tableland, where Post No 2 may be established.

As far as it can at present be determined, it is proposed that an *entrepot* for provisions shall be formed, and a brigade stationed there, probably until the return of the expedition.

Much more value is attached to the attainment of a convenient point of debarkation, and of an easy march to the healthy and cooler highland through a tract supplied with water and forage, than to any saving of distance by striking the probable line of advance a little further on in the direction of our march to the capital of Theodore.

There will be little value in a gain of distance which shall detain our troops in the low land, as it is not proposed to take any but pack carriage beyond Post No 2, up to which point, however, it is proposed to open a cart-road for artillery and stores, as soon as it may be possible.

It is to be remembered that it will be necessary to establish and provision several posts of considerable strength, to maintain the communications, and that during the passage of the force the connecting roads will be improved. It would be inconvenient to expend this labour on a line which would be untenable in the hot weather, and to be liable to shift the connecting posts during the operations.

With reference to the communication between the landing-place and the highland, it will probably not be difficult to find a track which, taking advantage of any natural facilities of the country, may be made possible for wheeled carriages with moderate labour, while a more direct route might be found for pack carriage.

After the foregoing and general points have been considered and disposed of, the officers of the Engineers and Quartermaster-General's department should make a rapid reconnaissance of the country for a space of from five to ten miles radius from the landing-place, according to the nature of the ground, and prepare such sketches of the routes as they can make without too great a detention.

It is, of course, desirable that the reconnaissance should be extended as far into the highland of Abyssinia as may be practicable, but in this matter Colonel Merewether will be guided by his knowledge of the country, so as not to compromise the safety of any of his party.

It is desirable that the first examination should be made at Annesley Bay, because it is the nearest point, and there will have been less time for the proceedings of the party to attract attention in the country.

It is necessary that someone well acquainted with the different descriptions of forage should accompany the expedition, to report on the quality of that which may be met with, sufficient samples of which might be brought down to the landing-place.

R. NAPIER.

Schedule of Marches from
Zula to Magdala

Stage	Distance	Cumulative Mileage
ZULA	—	—
KUMAYLI	14	14
SURU	13	27
UNDUL WELLS	13	40
RARA GUDI	17	57
SENAFÉ	9	66
GUNA-GUNA	12	78
FOCADA	14	92
ADIGRAT	14	106
MAI-WAHEZ	14	120
ADA BAGA	17	137
DONGOLO	10	147
AGULA	10	157
DOLO	16	173
EIKHULLET	9	182
ANTALO	12	194
MASGAH	9	203
MASHIK	8	211
ATSALA	10	221
BULAGO	9	230
MAKAN	6	236
ASHANGI	14	250
MUSSAGITA	8	258
LAT	7	265
MARAWAH	10	275
DILDI	14	289

WANDACH	8	297
MUJA	6	303
TAKAZZE	6	309
SANTARA	4	313
GAHSO	11	324
SINDI	18	342
BETHOR	7	349
JEDDA RAVINE	6	355
DALENTA	9	364
BESHILO RAVINE	15	369
MAGDALA	12	381

Note: Mileages vary slightly from one account to the other. These are taken from the Official Record, but have been rounded off to the nearest mile.

Magdala Today

In 1968, the centenary of Napier's expedition to Magdala, Stephen Bell and John Fynn, two undergraduates, were able to visit Zula and most of the British route to Magdala. They found that the country had changed but little, and were able to examine many relics of the campaign.

Napier was not the only commander to see the strategic value of Annesley Bay as a harbour. Traces of ancient Greek civilization may be found, while a great many concrete floors are the only remains of 400 huts built by the Italian army, and destroyed by the British in 1940. On the waterfront, a little to the south of the Italian pier, are the remains of the pier built by the Indian Engineers for the transference of men and materials from Napier's ships. The first hundred yards of the railway is clearly indicated by the growth of shrubs and bushes, which will only survive the fierce winds if their roots are embedded in the compressed foundations of the railway.

For five miles inland the river Hadas has obliterated all traces of the railway; beyond this cuttings and embankments, lined with bushes, become a predominant feature, showing the railway route right up to Kumayli. Fynn and Bell found the stone abutments of the two-span bridge in good condition, however, the girders and all other useful pieces of iron had been carried off to make guns for the Italians. One railway axle had, however, survived this pilfering—it required three people to stand it on end, recalling the complaints of members of the expedition as to the clumsiness of the rolling-stock.

It was impossible to explore the railway terminal owing to the presence of political 'shifta', occupying areas between Zula and Senafé and causing much disruption. These 'shifta' are fighting for the independence of Eritrea and very much resent the Amhara rule which governs Ethiopia.

Napier's route to Senafé was easy to follow, although beyond Senafé parts of it had been destroyed by the retreating troops and the area was occupied by 'shifta'. The most interesting relic in Senafé is the graveyard, which contains the graves of six British soldiers from the expedition, including that of Colonel Dunn, VC, who was killed by accident while out on a partridge shoot. Bell and Fynn were able to identify all the garrison and supply posts between Senafé and Lake Ashangi, where Napier's force, sticking to the high ground, veered to the west of the main Addis Ababa road. The local inhabitants have taken advantage of the defensive positions built by the British and in many places have built on top of them; the Italian fort at Adigrat owes its position to the British encampment on which it is built.

Bell and Fynn walked to Magdala from Dessie, and were well rewarded by the spectacular appearance of Theodore's mountain stronghold. Since 1868 and its abandonment Magdala, locked by rugged mountains and seldom visited by strangers, has returned to oblivion among its fellow hills. But there still lives on the plateau the grandson of Theodore's smith, who built guns and forged the shackles of the prisoners. There, too, was the deacon of the only church, whose grandfather had carried the keys for Theodore, and whose father had been a great friend of Theodore's son, Alamayu, who was taken to England by the retiring army for an education. 'Sebastopol', Theodore's giant mortar, still lay on top of the rise over which the British were to come, still magnificent despite the cracked breech. The Emperor's road, built for transporting 'Sebastopol' to Magdala, was just discernible, while four smaller mortars lay in the gullies into which they had been toppled from the mountain. Kokit Bir Gate is ruined, but the steps to it are in good order; while opinions vary widely as to the position of Theodore's grave in the shambolic ruins of the graveyard. No buildings survived Napier's ransacking, barely any foundations can be discerned, though the cut in the rock at the only path, made so that it could be defended by one man, is plainly visible.

Curiously, no local legends seem to have sprung up about the campaign. One old man gave an imitation of the mahouts swaying on the necks of their elephants which his grandmother had described to him. This was the first and last time that tame elephants had visited that part of Abyssinia; it is amazing that a description of an actual event should survive without legends, or indeed, any embellishment.

BIBLIOGRAPHY

Letters from Abyssinia, A Staff Officer (Lt. Scott)
Reconnoitring in Abyssinia, Wilkins
British Captives in Abyssinia, Beke
The British Expedition to Abyssinia, Hozier
Ten Years with King Theodore, Waldmeier
The Abyssinian Expedition, Markham
Magdala and Coomassie, Stanley
The Abyssinian Expedition, Shepherd
Record of the Expedition to Abyssinia, Holland and Hozier
"Correspondence on the Abyssinia War", Napier (W. O. Library)
Letters of Field Marshal Lord Napier, Napier
Life of Lord Napier of Magdala, Napier
"Further Papers connected with the Abyssinian Expedition", Blue Book
Official Journal of the Reconnaissance Party, Phayre
"Report by the Select Committee on the Abyssinian War", House of Commons Papers
The British Mission to Theodore, Rassam
Captive in Abyssinia, Blanc
London Gazette 1868
History of the Royal Artillery, Headlam
I Serve (History of the 3rd Dragoon Guards), Oatts
The Kings Own, Cowper
History of the 33rd Foot, Lee
The Sherwood Foresters, Wylie
Diary of Captain Hayward (published in The Sherwood Foresters Regimental Annual 1927)
History of the Sikh Pioneers, McMunn

41 Years in India, Roberts

Lord Roberts, James

Victorian Military Campaigns, Bond (Editor)

Constitutional History of India 1600–1935, Keith

"Indian Army Lists 1867–1900"

"Government of India Act 1858"

A History of Abyssinia, Jones & Monroe

"Notes on the life of W. A. Wynter, Ensign, 33rd, in the Abyssinian Campaign", Compiled by his son, Brig H. W. Wynter, DSO (unpublished)

"Napier of Magdala MSS", "Rassam Donation", "John Lawrence Donation", India Office Library

History of the British Army, Fortescue

Battles of the British Army, Low

British Battles and Medals, Gordon

INDEX